Mutual Funds

How to Simplify your Financial Life
and
Beat the Pro's

Dale C. Maley

Artephius Publishing

Index Mutual Funds:

How to Simplify your Financial Life and Beat the Pro's

By Dale C. Maley

Published By: Artephius Publishing
1291 Latham Drive
Watkinsville, GA 30677

Copyright © 1999 by Dale C. Maley
First Printing 1999
Printed in the United States of America

ISBN 0-9667052-0-3

Library of Congress Catalog Card Number: 98-96634

Table of Contents

Bull Market in Stocks • Global
Competition and 401(K)'s • Anticipated
Demise of the Social Security System
• Baby Boomers • Lack of Investor
Knowledge • Low Barriers to Entry
• Future of Mutual Funds

Best Type of Investment Asset • Are
Common Stocks Too Risky?
• Diversification • A Professionally
Managed Mutual Fund is Born
• Continued Popularity of Mutual Funds

Appendix

About The Author

Dale C. Maley is a very successful private investor who has been a student of Financial Planning and Investing for over 20 years. He was trained as an engineer at the University of Illinois and has been a practicing engineer for 20 years. His accomplishments as an engineer include granting of 14 U.S. Patents and authorship of over 100 professional technical papers. He is also a member of the International Society of Automotive Engineers and the Society of Manufacturing Engineers.

He also has earned an MBA (Masters Degree in Business Administration) degree from Illinois State University. His background in mathematics, engineering, and business provides him with the excellent basis for understanding and teaching investments and financial planning.

He is a very successful investor who has been investing in common stocks and mutual funds since 1980. He has also personally invested in both 401(K) and IRA plans, so he is familiar with participation and management of these types of investments. He has been investing in indexed common stock mutual funds since 1990.

Acknowledgment

I have not attempted to cite in the text all the authorities and sources that were consulted for preparation of this book. To do so would require more space than is available. The list would include departments of the Federal Government, libraries, institutions, and many periodicals.

Every effort has been made to trace, contact, and obtain permission from copyright holders for any copyrighted materials used in this book. However, in some instances, this has proved to be impossible. If notified, the publisher will be pleased to rectify any omissions in the next edition of this book.

Many friends helped review and improve the book. I would particularly like to thank Don Harris, Whiteford Mauldin, Chuck Twiggs, Wes James, and Jim Munz for their help and support.

I would like to thank Professor William Scott of the Illinois State University College of Business. I learned a great deal from Professor Scott's classes on investment and finance. Through a term paper in Professor Scott's class, I was able to first learn about the advantages of indexing compared to professional portfolio management.

Many thanks also go to Matthew Roberts, President of Index Funds Online. Matthew provided support and inspiration for completing this book.

I would also like to thank my wife Connie for her understanding and support in writing this book.

Warning-Disclaimer

This book is designed to provide information in regard to the subject matter covered. It is sold with the understanding that the publisher and author are not engaged in rendering legal, accounting or other professional services. If legal or other expert assistance is required, the services of a competent professional should be sought.

It is not the purpose of this manual to reprint all the information that is otherwise available to the author and/or publisher, but to complement, amplify, and supplement other texts. You are urged to read all the available material, learn as much as possible about investing and to tailor the information to your individual needs. For more information, see the many references in the Appendix.

Investing is not a get-rich-scheme. Anyone who decides to invest must expect to contribute a lot of time and effort.

Every effort has been made to make this book as complete and as accurate as possible. However, there **may be mistakes** both typographical and in content. Therefore, this text should be used only as a general guide and not as the ultimate of investing information. Furthermore, this book contains information on investing only up to the printing date.

The purpose of this book is to educate and entertain. The author and Artephius Publishing shall have neither liability nor responsibility to any person or entity with respect to any loss or damage caused, or alleged to be caused, directly or indirectly by the information contained in this book.

If you do not wish to be bound by the above, you may return this book to the publisher for a full refund.

Chapter 1

Mutual Fund Shock

Many people only buy a new car every five or ten years. When these people walk onto the car dealer's lot after being out of the new car market for many years, they are shocked by how much the cost of new cars has increased!

This same type of "shock" is experienced by new mutual fund investors. A new mutual fund investor will often decide to investigate mutual fund investment by turning to the financial section of a newspaper. The new mutual fund investor is shocked to discover there are over 8,000 different mutual funds to choose from!! The new mutual fund investor is often completely overwhelmed about how to begin to choose from 8,000 different mutual funds.

A new investor often only has enough money to invest in one mutual fund. Once new investors learn they must pick only one mutual fund out of more than 8,000 funds, they quickly start to feel like players in a Russian roulette game!!

This book will help new investors make sense of the mutual fund industry. New investors will learn why there are so many mutual funds available. This book will also explain the basics of mutual funds and common stock index mutual funds. The new investor will learn how to avoid having to sort through 8,000+ mutual funds by using a few common stock index funds to achieve their financial goals.

If you already invest in mutual funds, this book will show you how to beat 80% of the funds every year by using common stock indexed funds. You will learn how to evaluate the performance of your professionally managed mutual fund. You will learn how to determine if your professional mutual fund manager is really doing a good job with your investments.

The following chapter will simplify your financial life and let you achieve better results than 80% of the professional mutual fund managers!!

Most investors, both institutional and individual, will find that the best way to own common stocks is through an index fund that charges minimal fees. Those following this path are sure to beat the net results (after fees and expenses) delivered by the great majority of investment professionals.

-- Warren Buffett, in his 1996 Annual Berkshire Hathaway
    Report

Chapter 2

Why Are There Over 8,000 Mutual Funds to Choose From?

If you open up your newspaper to the financial section, you will find over 8,000 mutual funds to choose from for your investments!

When Congress passed the Investment Company Act of 1940, there were only 68 funds with a total of $448 million in assets. By 1998, the mutual fund industry had grown to over 8,000 funds with $4.5 trillion in assets!!

There are now more than 3,500 common stock mutual funds alone for investors to choose from!!

> *There are now more mutual funds than there are stocks listed on the New York Stock Exchange!*

There are many reasons why the number of mutual funds has exploded:

Bull Market in Stocks

The 1960's were a golden decade for stock market investment. After World War II, war torn Europe and Japan had to rebuild their industries. In the 1950's and 1960's, U.S. companies had no competition from European or Japanese companies. U.S. companies were able to dominate world markets. The U.S. stock market reflected the global success of its companies and it rose throughout the decade.

The 1970's, with oil embargoes and high inflation, was one of the worst decades in this century for common stock investment. Investors flocked out of the stock market into gold, Chinese antiques, and other items that held their value during highly inflationary times. In 1979, the cover of *Business Week* magazine even announced "The Death of Equities". *Business Week* was predicting the U.S. stock market was dead forever due to high inflation.

The 1980's ushered in the longest running Bull Market of the 20th Century. Low inflation, low interest rates, and improved corporate efficiency triggered and maintained this Bull Market. As investors realized the stock market was again a good place to invest, the demand for mutual funds increased dramatically.

The 1990's turned out to be just as good as the 1980's for U.S. stock market investors. Low interest rates, low inflation, and the success of large U.S. companies in global markets fueled the Bull Market.

The tremendous growth the stock market experienced can be shown by plotting the stock market at the end of each decade and ignoring yearly fluctuations:

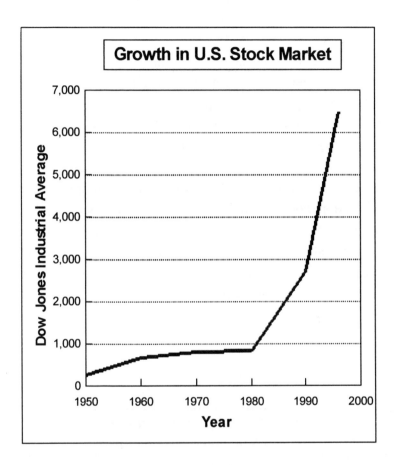

This tremendous growth in the U.S. stock market caused investors to demand more mutual funds so they could participate in the great Bull Market.

Global Competition and 401(K)'s

A traditional source of retirement income is a company's pension plan. Twenty or thirty years ago, many companies provided a defined benefit type pension plan for their employees.

A defined benefit pension plan means the employer provides a defined amount of pension benefits at your retirement. Typically, the employee might work for 30 years and then retire from the company. The company is responsible for setting aside enough company funds and investing them wisely such that the company can pay the employee a monthly pension. If the employee retires before the time period required to obtain the full pension, the company adjusts the amount of pension received based upon actual years worked. The employee has to take no actions under this system, except work the required number of years to qualify for the pension.

---

*Are you covered by a **defined benefits** or a **defined contribution** plan where you work?*

If you don't know, you need to see your Human Resources Department right away and find out!!

Over the last 20 years, companies have experienced many changes in their operating environments. Global competition, instead of just domestic competition, has caused companies to become more efficient so they can compete globally. The need to become globally competitive has caused many companies to take the following actions:

- *Reduce operating costs.* The company lowers its costs by laying-off employees. One example would be to reduce research and development costs by laying-off some research personnel.

- *Combine companies.* Companies combine to reduce the amount of overhead required to produce a product. When two banks combine, they often close some of the branches in the same city to reduce overhead costs. Reduction in overhead costs usually involves laying-off employees.

- *Reduce costs using technology.* Companies reduce cost by investing in new technology which can cause lay-offs. One example would be replacing human telephone operators with computers.

- *Reduce long term liabilities.* Companies do not want to be saddled with long term liabilities such as defined benefit pension plans. Companies reduce defined benefit pension plans and replace them with defined contribution plans. Under defined contribution plans, the company is only obligated to contribute a certain amount of money to each employee's retirement fund each year. Upon retirement, the employee does not receive a defined amount each month. The employee receives whatever their retirement fund can pay out based upon the return of the fund.

The result of these changes is that the number of defined benefit pension plans offered by companies has been dramatically reduced. About one-half of all working Americans have no company retirement plan of any type!!

Companies now offer defined contribution plans that are dependent on what return the funds earn during the employee's working life. Many employees lose a portion or all of their pension due to layoffs.

Although most laid-off employees do find new jobs, they still lose some or all of the pension benefits accrued at their previous employer.

A form of defined contribution pension plan that does help with the problem of changing employers and losing pension benefits is the 401(K) plan. Created by the Federal Government, this plan lets employees contribute their pretax dollars to a retirement fund. The employer will often contribute funds to this account also. If the employee changes jobs, the employee is allowed to transfer this account to his new employer, or cash out the fund with some tax liabilities.

With a 401(K) plan, the employee, not the company, is responsible for managing the type of investments made. The 401(K) plan does help employees who work for many different companies during their working career. They can take their 401(K) account with them each time they change jobs.

The traditional company pension plan can no longer be counted upon to be a reliable source of retirement income. Many companies have switched to defined contribution plans that do not pay a guaranteed monthly pension. Employees realize they need to contribute to their 401(K) plans. As of the end of 1996, 401(K) plans had grown to include 24 million participants holding $810 billion in investments!!

Most 401(K) plans use mutual funds for investments. This move away from traditional company pension plans to 401(K)'s has caused an increased demand for mutual funds.

Recent studies have shown that a young person entering the work force for the first time will work for an average of 8 different companies!

Thank goodness for 401(K) plans!! The "portability" of 401(K) plans will provide these workers with some retirement income.

Anticipated Demise of the Social Security System

Social Security is becoming a much less reliable source of retirement income for future recipients. The American public has lost faith in the future of the Social Security system. Recent polls have shown that more Americans believe in UFO's than believe in the future of Social Security!

A fundamental flaw with the Social Security program is that it is *not* a savings and investment plan. Since its conception, Social Security has been a *"pay as you go"* program. Money is collected from the employer and employee every time a paycheck is issued. This money is not invested by individual then paid to that same individual at retirement. The money is instead immediately paid out to current recipients of Social Security.

This "pay as you go" scheme worked during the first 50 years of the Social Security program. It worked because there were many more workers contributing to the program than there were recipients taking money out of the program. Because of surpluses in the program, Congress even expanded the eligibility of recipients. This increased eligibility resulted in more money being paid out of the program.

If we were directed from Washington when to sow and when to reap, we would soon want for bread. -- Thomas Jefferson

During the next 30 years, the Social Security program will run out of money to pay recipients. The ratio of workers to recipients will fall dramatically because so many Baby Boomers will be retiring.

Back in 1950, there were 16 workers for every recipient. In 1996, there were about 3 workers for each recipient. By 2030, there will only be 2 workers for every recipient. Under the current Social Security system, there are not enough workers supporting recipients.

It is projected the Social Security program will become bankrupt sometime in the next 10 to 30 years. To avoid bankruptcy of the program, the Federal Government will have to take some of the following actions:

- *Raise the retirement age.* You will have to wait several years longer to begin collecting benefits.

- *Increase taxes.* You and your employer will have to pay more taxes to the Social Security program.

- *Reduce benefits to the wealthy.* If you are successful and wealthy, you will be denied benefits.

- *Privatize the program.* As Chile or other countries have done, the program will be converted from a "pay as you go" system to a personal investment system. Your contributions will be invested in your own specific investment account.

It has become obvious to most people they probably will not receive the level of Social Security benefits that today's recipients are receiving. This uncertainty about the future of the Social Security system has prompted people to save for their retirement using mutual funds. This has created more demand for mutual funds.

Baby Boomers

After World War II, soldiers returning from war got married and triggered the largest wave of births ever seen in the United States. The babies born between 1946 and 1964 were nicknamed the Baby Boom generation. The Baby Boom generation is 67 million people strong!

The Baby Boom generation has caused major upheavals in every area of society they have encountered. In the late 1940's and early 1950's, Gerber could hardly keep up with the increased demand for baby food caused by this wave of infants.

In the 1950's and 1960's, school districts across the U.S. had to scramble to build new schools fast enough to provide classrooms for all these children.

In the 1970's and 1980's, the Baby Boomers started to get married and formed households. They proceeded to drive up the price of housing to new levels because these new families needed a place to live.

In 1986, the oldest of the Baby Boomers reached their 40th birthday. Some of these Boomers started to think about retirement and started to save and invest.

In 1996, the oldest Boomers hit 50 years of age. As they arrived at the milestone age of 50, more and more of them started to save and invest for retirement.

David Cork and Susan Lightstone, in their book *The Pig and the Python: How To Prosper From The Aging Baby Boom*, have done an excellent job describing the impact of the Baby Boomers. Based upon the Law of Supply and Demand, they show how the huge demand from the Boomers has exceeded the available supply of everything this generation has needed.

The Law of Supply and Demand is a simple one.
If demand exceeds supply, the price will rise.
If supply exceeds demand, the price will fall.

It is often said that through the centuries no politician has been able to repeal the Law of Supply and Demand!

Cork and Lightstone predict Baby Boomers will put some of their savings into investments like CD's (Certificates of Deposit). They predict this will cause interest rates to stay relatively low the next 20 years.

When Baby Boomers look for investments for their retirement funds, they will be forced to invest in the U.S. stock market. They will be forced into the stock market because returns from fixed return investments like CD's will be too low to give meaningful results.

Cork and Lightstone predict the 67 million Baby Boomers will put a tremendous demand upon the U.S. stock market for their retirement investments. They predict this situation will cause the U.S. stock market to rise dramatically for at least the next 20 years.

This huge demand for mutual funds from the Baby Boomers has caused the mutual fund industry to expand the number of funds available to try to meet the demands of this new market.

Lack of Investor Knowledge

Unfortunately, American schools do not teach people how to save and invest their money. American schools are primarily designed to teach people how to become good employees and good citizens. American schools teach you the skills needed to get a job and to earn money. The schools do not teach how to save or invest your money.

When people realize they need to invest to reach their long term goals, they don't know how to choose where to invest their money. An example of this is where an employee decides to start investing for retirement using the company's 401(K) plan. The employee goes to the Human Resources office and is given a brochure showing what mutual funds are available. The employee has no idea how to evaluate each different fund and choose a fund for his 401(K).

Many investors receive small "doses" of education from the newspaper, television, or books. They may hear or read about various experts who advocate specific investment methods.

Examples of the many different possible investments that investors hear about include:

- Bonds
- Certificates of Deposit (CD's)
- Commodities
- Dogs of the Dow Theory
- Dow Theory
- Foreign Stocks
- Futures
- Growth Investing
- Initial Public Offerings (IPO's)
- Junk Bonds
- Large Company Stocks
- Market Timing
- Money Market Funds
- Mutual Funds
- Sector Investing
- Small Company Stocks
- Technical Analysis

- Value Investing
- Market Neutral Mutual Funds
- Real Estate
- Gold
- Limited Partnerships

The education of a man is never completed until he dies. -
Robert E. Lee

Numerous studies have indicated how financially naive most American investors really are.

Money Magazine and Vanguard Group conducted one such study in 1997. They randomly chose 1,555 investors from across the United States. They asked them twenty basic questions regarding investing.

The investors got an "F" grade!! Even experienced investors only achieved an average grade of 64 out of 100.

Both Money Magazine and Vanguard often offer tests and educational material about investing. You may want to visit their web sites to check your own investment acumen!!

http://www.money.com

http://www.vanguard.com

> *Learning is a treasure that will follow its owner everywhere.* - Chinese Proverb

Because very few investors have had the opportunity to receive any formal education regarding investment, they do not know how to evaluate investments. They may demand mutual funds that invest in small company stocks because they heard somewhere that small companies perform better than large companies. This lack of investor knowledge has caused the mutual fund industry to create many different types of funds to meet the *perceived* needs of investors.

Low Barriers to Entry

In the 1980's, a business professor named Michael Porter, studied competition in the market place. One of the factors he identified was called "barriers to entry". He noted that if there are no tough barriers to overcome, many competitors will easily enter new lucrative markets. He noted that competitors do not enter lucrative markets if the barriers to entering that market are relatively high.

An example of an industry with very high barriers to entry would be the automotive industry. Starting a new car company would require billions of dollars of investment. Complying with all the government safety and emission regulations would also be very difficult.

An example of an industry with very low barriers to entry would be a food stand on a city street. Very little capital investment is required. Complying with government regulations is relatively easy if the proper permits are obtained.

The barriers to entering the mutual fund market are very low. Not much initial investment is required and governmental regulations are not difficult to overcome. Because so many new mutual funds are being created, consultant companies have sprung up to assist in the creation of new funds. Some consultants charge less than $50,000 to register a new fund. This is fairly inexpensive considering it will cost you about $1 million to buy a McDonald's restaurant franchise!!

These relatively low barriers to entry have allowed the number of funds offered to dramatically increase.

The Future of Funds

The future of mutual funds is hard to predict. Several possible scenarios may occur.

Under the first scenario, the number of funds available may continue to grow as it has in the past. The huge number of Baby Boomers saving for retirement, coupled with their lack of investment knowledge, may drive the number of funds to expand to meet their perceived needs.

In the second scenario, the number of funds available may decline. Small, unprofitable funds may be consolidated into larger, more profitable funds.

In the third scenario, indexed funds will continue to gain in popularity as investors understand the inherent advantages of indexed funds. This shift in assets from professionally managed funds to indexed funds may cause the smaller unprofitable managed funds to be consolidated with the larger and more profitable managed funds.

In the fourth scenario, the U.S. Congress could change the shape of the entire mutual fund industry. Congress could decide to privatize the Social Security system. Congress could allow investors to invest their money in a very limited number of government run mutual funds. These funds could include one common stock index fund, one bond index fund, and one money market fund. It is hard to predict what impact government run mutual funds would have on the current mutual fund industry.

In a fifth scenario, the U.S. Congress could privatize the Social Security system, but would allow investors to put their Social Security money into existing mutual funds. This huge new flow of money into the mutual fund industry would probably cause the number of mutual funds to increase dramatically.

In the following chapters of this book, you will learn the inherent advantages of using indexed funds as compared to using professionally managed funds. My hope for you is that after reading this book, you will be one of the participants who help indexed funds gain in popularity over professionally managed funds.

The best way to predict the future is
to invent it. -- Alan Kay

Chapter 3

Basics of Mutual Funds

It is extremely important to have a full understanding why mutual funds were created and how they work.

We will explain how mutual funds originated and how they work by following the story of a fictitious investor named Jill. At the time of Jill's story, mutual funds have not been invented yet.

Jill is a serious investor who only has $5,000 to invest to achieve her long term goals. She will be investing her money for at least five years. She has never invested in anything except her bank savings account. Jill has never had an opportunity to study investing.

Jill's nephew, Ned, is just finishing a four year degree in Business. Ned's favorite classes in college were Finance and Investments. Ned learned about the stock market when he was 13 years old and joined the Stock Market Club at school. In the Stock Market Club, his team always did the best job of figuring out which stocks to buy and sell. He studied Finance and Investments in college so he could learn more about the stock market. Ned does not have a job lined up yet, but is planning on working in a field related to the stock market.

Jill's daughter has a friend in school. The father of this friend is William. William is a Professor of Finance at State University. Jill has visited with William while they watched their daughters play together on the school soccer team. William has studied the stock market a great deal, but has never invested any of his money in the stock market.

Best Type of Investment Asset

As Jill started the process of investing her money, she wondered where she should invest her funds to get the best return on her investment. She had heard about stocks and bonds, but never had a chance to study them.

She decided to call William, the Finance Professor. William told her that common stocks have always given the highest rate of return over alternative types of investments. He also told Jill that common stocks can be divided into categories such as large and small company common stocks.

William told her that a company called Ibbotson Associates had studied the returns of various asset types over the last 70 years. William sent Jill the results of Ibbotson's research:

Type of Investment	Annual Rate of Return Over Last 70 Years
Large Company U.S. Common Stocks	10.70%
Small Company U.S. Common Stocks	12.60%
Corporate Bonds	5.60%
U.S. Treasury Bonds	5.10%
U.S. Treasury Bills	3.70%

Ibbotson Associates publishes an annual yearbook which documents historical asset returns.
Check out Ibbotson's web site at www.Ibottson.com

After studying Ibbotson's results, Jill noted that common stocks have historically given higher returns to investors than bonds or Treasury Bills. Jill now understood that common stocks have historically given the highest returns. She was nervous about investing in the stock market because she had heard it was very risky. She remembered hearing sometimes about bad days for the stock market on the evening television news.

Are Common Stocks Too Risky?

After studying Ibottson's chart, Jill wanted to invest in common stocks , but she thought she might lose all her money in the stock market.

Jill decided to give William the Finance Professor another call. She asked William if common stocks were too risky.

William told Jill that most studies have shown that as long as you are investing for at least 5 years, the stock market should give the highest return on her investment. He told her that for investment periods less than 5 years, safer investments such as bonds or Treasury Bills should be used. The return on common stocks is too volatile for periods less than 5 years.

> *There are two times in a man's life when he should*
> *not speculate: when he can't afford*
> *it, and when he can.* -- Mark Twain

William also told Jill the more risk she is willing to take with her investment, the higher the return she can achieve. He also told her she was guaranteed to lose money after inflation and taxes if she chose low risk investments like U.S. Treasury Bills.

William agreed to send Jill a chart showing the relationship between risk and reward. He also agreed to send her an example of what happens after the effects of inflation and taxes on low risk investments.

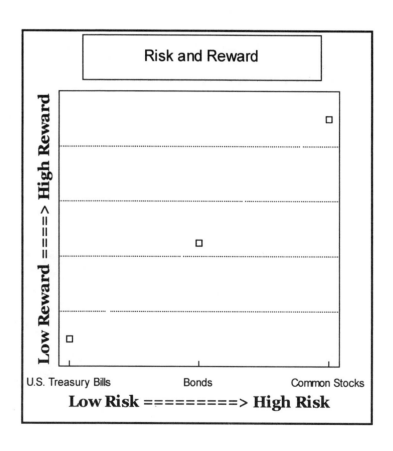

Jill studied William's risk and reward chart. She noted that if you are willing to take on more risk, you can get a higher reward or return on your investment.

Jill then studied William's example of what happens to low risk investments after the effects of inflation and taxes:

Returns After Inflation and Taxes

For example, you decide to invest in a Certificate of Deposit that pays you 5% interest per year. If you are in a 28% tax bracket and inflation runs 4% per year, after taxes and inflation your return will be:

Return of C.D. =	+5.0%
Taxes = 28% of 5% =	-1.4%
Inflation = 4% =	-4.0%
	+ ____
Net Return =	-0.40%

So after factoring in the effects of taxes and inflation, your 5% interest rate on the Certificate of Deposit becomes a negative rate of return!!!

Common stocks have historically returned about 10% per year.

Let's examine what happens if you decide to invest in a common stock mutual fund that averages a 10% return per year. If you are in a 28% tax bracket and inflation runs 4% per year, after taxes and inflation your return will be:

Return of Mutual Fund =	+10.00%
Taxes = 28% of 10% =	- 2.80%
Inflation = 4% =	- 4.0%
	+ ____
Net Return =	+ 3.2%

So after factoring in the effects of taxes and inflation, your 10% return on the common stock mutual fund becomes a positive 3.2% rate of return. This means you are increasing the value of your investment each year.

After reviewing the information from William, Jill decided that low risk investments are really guaranteed to lose money after inflation and taxes. Jill decided she should invest her $5,000 in common stocks so she could grow her investment after inflation and taxes.

Diversification

As Jill was preparing to select which common stocks to buy, a thought occurred to her. If she only invested in the stock of one company, that company could encounter rough times and could even go bankrupt. If the company she invested in declared bankruptcy, she would lose all of her money!!

Jill wondered if she should invest in more than one stock to reduce her risk of a company going bankrupt. She remembered her mother telling her she should never "put all her eggs in one basket".

Jill called William again and told him about her concern about bankruptcy if she invested in only one company. She also told him about her idea of not putting all her eggs in one basket.

William laughed at her comment about **not** putting all her eggs into one basket! William told her she was exactly right about not putting all her eggs into one basket. William told her that financial experts had a fancy name for this called diversification. He told her she needed to invest in 15 or 20 different stocks to reduce her risk. He also said that after about 20 different stocks, it did not do any good to buy more different stocks. William sent Jill a chart which demonstrated how her risk would be reduced by increasing the number of different stocks she bought:

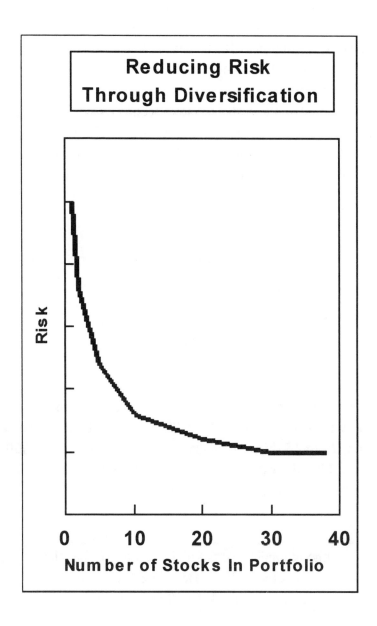

After studying William's chart, Jill decided she needed to buy at least 25 different stocks to stay diversified. Jill had also done a little research about stock brokers and discovered that unless she bought at least 100 shares of a stock, brokerage fees for buying or selling the stock would be excessive. Jill decided she would buy 100 shares of 25 different stocks.

Jill looked in the financial section of her newspaper and noticed most stocks sell between $25 and $75 per share. Jill decided the average stock would cost around $50.00 per share. Jill calculated what it would cost to buy 100 shares of 25 different stocks:

25 stocks x 100 shares x $50.00 average cost
per share

= $125,000

Jill was shocked to discover that to be diversified she would need at least $125,000!! Even if she dropped from 25 to 15 different stocks, she will still need $75,000!! Since Jill only had $5,000 to invest, it appeared she would not be able to invest in common stocks.

Although most stocks sell for $25 to $75 per share, Warren Buffett's Berkshire-Hathaway stock listed for $45,000 per share in late 1997 !!

A Professionally Managed Mutual Fund is Born

Jill wanted to invest in U.S. common stocks, but she did not have enough money to adequately diversify. Jill had not seen her nephew Ned for a while. She decided to visit Ned and discuss her problem with investing in common stocks.

Jill arranged a meeting with her nephew Ned, who was finishing his degree in Business at State University. Ned told Jill he would be trying to find a job where he got to choose which stocks to buy and sell because he really liked picking stocks. Ned told her he did not have any money to buy and sell his own stocks.

Jill told Ned about her problem of not having enough money to invest in common stocks. After discussing their mutual problems for a while, Ned came up with a brainstorm idea. He suggested that Jill, plus many other small investors like her, pool their money together so they had enough to adequately diversify. Ned could then manage the money and do what he did best, select which stocks to buy and sell. Ned thought this idea solved the Jill's problem of not having enough money to diversify. It also solved his problem of not having any money to invest with.

> *Our life is frittered away by detail. Simplicity, simplicity, simplicity!*
> --Henry David Thoreau

Jill really liked Ned's idea. She told him he could handle all the paperwork involved with buying and selling stocks. If Ned would take care of this paperwork, all the small investors like Jill would have much easier record-keeping. Jill wanted the simplest record-keeping possible.

Ned pointed out he would have some expenses. These expenses would include advertising to attract investors, brokerage fees, his salary, and a little profit. Ned said he could recoup those costs by charging each investor a per cent of their assets invested each year.

Ned did some quick calculating on the back of an envelope. He then told Jill the annual fee would be between 1% and 4% a year. He told her that as more people invested, the annual fee would probably drop. Ned told Jill he would make up a document called a prospectus that would spell out all the fees and rules for the enterprise.

Jill suggested that Ned call his new enterprise Ned's Mutual Fund since many investors were pooling their money into a fund which would mutually benefit all of them.

Continued Popularity of Mutual Funds

Jill's story above demonstrates why and how mutual funds were created. The very first mutual funds were created in the 1880's in Scotland. Scottish investors pooled their money together so they could invest in a thriving new country called the United States. The Scots called their pooled associations Investment Trusts.

Some of the companies that created these first Investment Trusts still exist today (see the Internet at http://www.sit.co.uk/company%20profile.htm).

Common stock mutual funds have continued to gain in popularity in the United States as shown in the chart below:

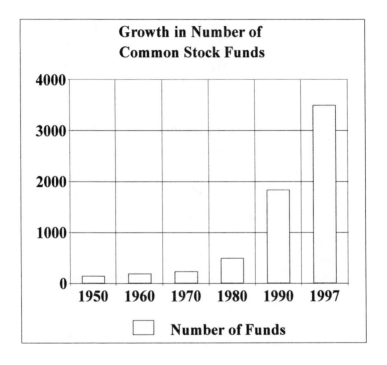

Mutual funds remain very popular because they provide investors with some very valuable benefits. These benefits include:

- Investors may not have the desire, time, training, or temperament to manage their own common stock portfolio. It is not easy to choose winning stocks from the over 15,000 stocks available! By pooling their investments, investors can afford to hire professional managers to oversee their investments.

- Investors may lack enough funds to diversify their investments to reduce risk. Investing in a mutual fund allows investors to diversify because funds typically own 40 to several thousand different common stocks.

- Investors can get convenience and service from mutual funds. Most funds offer automatic investment and redemption plans.

I am a great believer in luck. The harder I work the more of it I seem to have. -- Coleman Cox

---

- Mutual funds are very liquid markets. Investors can easily and quickly buy and sell mutual funds.

- Mutual funds allow investors to switch their investments from one type of fund to another if economic conditions change or the investor's objectives change.

- Mutual funds offer simplified accounting to the investor. The mutual fund takes care of all bookkeeping, issues periodic statements, and provides tax records.

> *The average mutual fund holds about 120 different stocks.*

Chapter 4

Mutual Fund Performance

We will continue with our fictitious character Jill to help explain how to determine mutual fund performance.

How to Know Your Mutual Fund is the Best

After Jill and her nephew Ned set up the first mutual fund, thousands of new mutual funds were created. After a couple of years investing in Ned's mutual fund, Jill started to wonder if some of these new funds were providing their investors with better returns than Ned's fund.

She wondered how she could determine if Ned's fund was the best fund to have her money invested in.

Since Ned was her nephew, she did not want to take a chance of making him mad at her by insinuating his management of her money was not good enough. She decided to call William the Finance Professor.

Fund Comparisons

Jill gave William a call. She asked William how she could determine which fund was the best. William told her there were a couple of different ways to make fund comparisons. He suggested she compare the annual performance of Ned's fund to other funds similar to Ned's. William told Jill that personal finance magazines like *Money* or *Kiplingers* often made these types of fund comparisons.

Jill asked William if she could compare Ned's fund to the over-all stock market performance. William told Jill that she could do this. He said the whole stock market can be represented by an index measure. William said one of the most popular indexes was the Standard & Poors 500, or S&P 500 as it is usually called. William sent Jill a list of some of the popular indexes used to represent the entire stock market:

Index Name	Description
Dow Jones Industrial	30 large U.S. stocks. The Dow Jones Company selects which stocks are included in the index.
S&P 500	500 large U.S. companies. Often called "Blue Chip" companies. Represents about 70% of the total value of all companies in the United States. The 500 companies in the index are not the 500 largest companies. This index is designed to simulate many different sectors of the U.S. economy. The index is composed of roughly 400 industrial, 40 utility, 40 financial, and 20 transportation stocks.
Wilshire 5,000	In 1971, when this index was first created, it included all of the 5,000 companies headquartered in the United States. Now, the index includes the over 7,000 companies with headquarters in the United States. This index represents almost 100% of the total value of all companies in the United States.

I've known people to spend more time comparison shopping for paper towels than for investments. -- SEC Chairman Arthur Levitt

William told Jill the Wilshire 5,000 was the index that covered almost all of the U.S. stock market. He told her the S&P 500 was also a popular benchmark because it covered 500 large companies which represented many different sectors of the U.S. economy.

William suggested Jill not use the Dow Jones Industrial Average for fund comparisons because it only follows 30 large companies. He told Jill he did not feel 30 companies was a broad enough index for the whole U.S. stock market.

Jill subscribed to a personal finance magazine and began to track the performance of Ned's mutual fund against both the Wilshire 5,000 and the S&P 500. She also tracked the performance of other successful funds against these two broad market indexes.

Education is not the filling of a pail, but the lighting of a fire. - William Butler Yeats

Chapter 5

Index Funds

W e will continue to use our fictitious investor Jill to help explain how and why index funds exist.

Mutual Funds Not Consistent

Jill monitored the performance of Ned's fund for several years. She also monitored similar common stock funds to see if they performed as well as the S&P 500.

After several years of monitoring mutual fund performance, Jill made some observations. One year Ned's fund did very well compared to the other funds. The other years Ned's fund did not do very well compared to the other funds.

Jill also noticed that each year a different set of mutual funds were the top performers. It seemed like no particular fund was able to consistently be the best year after year.

Jill noticed that every year, many funds were not able to match the performance of the S&P 500 index. Since the S&P 500 was an unmanaged index and the mutual funds were run by professionally trained managers, why couldn't all the mutual funds beat the performance of the S&P 500 every year??

Jill became confused. She wanted to make sure her money was invested with someone who gave her the best returns year after year. It appeared that no mutual fund could give her the best returns every year. She decided to call her friend William, the Finance Professor.

Fund Performance

Jill gave William a call. She explained to William her observations about mutual fund performance over the last several years. She asked William why all professional fund managers could not out-perform an unmanaged index like the S&P 500.

William was not able to answer Jill's questions. He told Jill he needed to do some further research. He told her he would get back to her in a couple of weeks with his findings.

Cost Disadvantage

William began to research the issue of fund managers not being able to beat the S&P 500 every year. The first thing William discovered was that a professionally managed common stock mutual fund has a major cost disadvantage to a fund indexed to the S&P 500. A professionally managed common stock mutual fund must charge each investor a per cent of their assets to cover various costs that an indexed fund does not have to pay. Examples of these types of expenses include:

- The cost of the professional fund manager(s). A fund manager can be paid anywhere from $100,000 to over $1 million per year. An indexed fund simply buys all the stocks in its index. Since an indexed fund does not need professional managers to select stocks to buy and sell, they do not have to pay these high management fees.

- The cost of research to determine which stocks to buy and sell. Many professionally managed funds have full time researchers to suggest to the professional manager which stocks to buy or sell. Some professionally managed funds pay outside research companies to do this research. Since an indexed fund simply buys all the stocks in the index, it does not have to do any research on what stocks to buy and sell.

- The cost of brokerage fees incurred whenever stocks are bought or sold. Professional fund managers buy and sell anywhere from 10% to over 100% of the common stocks in their portfolio each year. Every time the professional manager decides to buy or sell a stock in the hopes of improving the fund's return to its investors, the fund incurs brokerage fees. Since an index fund only buys and sells stocks when investors add money to the fund, or they want to redeem their shares in the fund, an index fund incurs a relatively small amount of brokerage fees.

The three examples above illustrate some of the additional costs a professionally managed common stock mutual fund must incur compared to an index fund. The professionally managed fund must charge its investors anywhere from 1% to 3% of the money the investor has invested in the fund. An indexed fund typically charges 0.2% to 1% of the investor's assets.

The average common stock mutual fund manager buys and sells 80% of the common stocks in the mutual fund each year !!

Since common stocks have historically returned 10% per year, an investor who participates in a professionally managed common stock fund would only receive 7% to 9% per year due to fund expenses:

10% Historical - 3% Fund Fees = 7% Net
Return of   Return
Common   to
Stocks   Investor

10% Historical - 1% Fund Fees = 9% Net
Return of   Return
Common   to
Stocks   Investor

An investor in a common stock mutual fund indexed to the S&P 500 with an annual expense ratio of 0.2% receives a much higher return than the investor in a professionally managed fund:

10%	-	0.2%	=	9.8%
Historical		Fund		Net
Return of		Fees		Return
Common				to
Stocks				Investor

At first glance, receiving a 9.8% return from an indexed fund compared to a 7% return from a professionally managed fund does **not** seem like that great of penalty. After all, this is only a difference of 2.8%.

As an investor, you want to maximize your return after the effects of inflation and taxes. Let us return to the example we studied earlier on how to calculate the return from common stocks after the effects of inflation and taxes:

Common Stock Returns After Inflation and Taxes

Common stocks have historically returned about 10% per year.

Let's examine what happens if you decide to invest in a common stock mutual fund that averages a 10% return per year. If you are in a 28% tax bracket and inflation runs 4% per year, after taxes and inflation your return will be:

Return of Mutual Fund =	+10.00%
Taxes = 28% of 10% =	- 2.80%
Inflation = 4% =	- 4.0%
	+
Net Return =	+ 3.2%

So after factoring in the effects of taxes and inflation, your 10% return on the common stock mutual fund becomes a positive 3.2% rate of return.

The 10% return on common stocks noted above can be achieved by a common stock fund indexed to the S&P 500, but such a fund has a minimum expense ratio of 0.2%.

Since we know you can achieve 3.2% after the effects of inflation and taxes, we can calculate how big of an impact the 0.2% expense ratio of an indexed fund has on your net return after inflation and taxes:

0.2% Expense of Indexed Fund   = 6.25%
3.2% Historical Return on Common Stocks

So, the index fund investor loses about 6.25% of his after-inflation and after-tax return of 10% due to the expenses incurred by the index fund. This is *not* a very significant factor.

Now, let us calculate the effect of the 3% expense ratio incurred by a professionally managed common stock fund:

3.0% Expense of Mutual Fund   = 94%
3.2% Historical Return on Common Stocks

So, the investor in the professionally managed common stock mutual fund *loses 94%* of his after-inflation and after-tax return of 10% due to the expenses incurred by the professionally managed common stock mutual fund!!

From a viewpoint of an investor concerned about his after-tax and after-inflation net return, index funds help an investor to achieve much higher net returns!! The higher expense ratios incurred by professionally managed common stock mutual funds *are a very big issue!*

If you calculate the impact this lower net return from professionally managed funds can have on long term investing, it also illustrates how big an issue this can be to investors. Let us illustrate this by examining two different investors. Both investors invest $10,000 and let it grow for 30 years. Investor one uses a professionally managed common stock mutual fund that yields him an after-tax after-inflation net return of 0.2% (3.2 % net return of common stocks minus 3.0% expense ratio). Investor two uses a common stock indexed mutual fund that yields him an after-tax after-inflation net return of 3.0% (3.2 % net return of common stocks minus 0.2% expense ratio). After 30 years of investing, each investor will have:

Value After 30 Years Using Professionally Managed Fund After Taxes and Inflation	Value After 30 Years Using Index Fund After Taxes and Inflation	Difference
$10,618	$24,273	$13,655

After 30 years, the investor who used the indexed fund had $13,655 *more* than the investor who used the professionally managed fund!!

Professionally managed common stock mutual funds do have a major cost disadvantage compared to indexed common stock funds. This cost differential can have a major affect on the returns achieved by investors.

Just to equal the return to investors from an indexed stock fund, professional fund managers must achieve returns higher than the market index to cover their higher fund costs. This often causes professional fund mangers to take even higher risks with their portfolio, which increases the risk taken by their investors compared to an index fund.

Efficient Market Theory

As William did some further research, he discovered a revolutionary theory called the Efficient Market Theory. This theory states the stock market is a fair game. Given the risk level of a particular stock, the odds of the stock giving the investor a future return higher than expected is exactly the same, 50%, as the odds of the stock giving the investor a future return lower than expected.

The theory also says there is no way for an investor to the use the information available at a given time in order to earn a return higher than expected. In the long run, stocks will return exactly what is expected. No investor can earn an abnormally high return!

William studied this theory further. He found the Efficient Market Theory is based on the principle the stock market is an efficient user of information. With more than 10,000 professionally trained financial analysts continuously studying the stock market, any new piece of information is immediately reflected in the price of stocks.

William found an ironic aspect about this theory. The U.S. stock market is one of the most intensely researched stock markets in the world. U.S. companies have to follow very thorough and consistent methods of reporting their financial information to the public. Therefore, there is a relatively large amount of information made available in a timely fashion to investors.

The minute new information is made available about a company, the professional financial analysts who follow that company adjust their recommendations of the company's stock price immediately. Investors, who rely on the recommendations of the financial analysists, immediately bid the stock price up or down based on the new information.

The ironic aspect of this phenomena is that the U.S. stock market is a relatively efficient user of new information because of the 10,000+ professional financial analysts. Without the financial analysts to continuously monitor companies and interpret how new information will affect a stock's price, investors would have a difficult time identifying stocks which will go up or down in value. With the presence of financial analysts, their analysis of the impact of new information on stock prices makes the market so efficient that no investor can consistently beat the market! Without the financial analysts, the stock market would be an inefficient user of new information, and some sharp investors might be able to use new information to beat the returns of the market!

William also found some information which indicated the Efficient Market Theory might not work as well for foreign stock markets as it does for the U.S. stock market. Many foreign stock markets do not have as many financial analysts monitoring the stock market as the U.S. does. Also, many foreign countries do not require as extensive and consistent disclosure by companies of information that could affect the price of their stock. Since not as much information is available on foreign stocks, the foreign stock markets may not be as efficient as the U.S. stock market. With the trend of global investing, foreign stock markets are moving towards the same information efficiency level as the U.S. stock market. Over time, foreign stock markets will approach the same market efficiency as the U.S. stock market.

Monkeys and Dart Boards

William thought about the Theory of Efficient Markets. If this theory is really true, a professional money manager should not do any better at picking winning stocks than a blindfolded monkey throwing darts at a dart board with a list of stocks attached to the dart board!!

William did some more research and discovered the interesting case of a U.S. Senator who tried out the dart board theory. Senator Thomas J. McIntyre of the Banking Committee, attached the stock market page to his dart board. The Senator then threw some darts at the dart board. It turned out the Senator's dart board stock selections beat almost all the mutual funds over the time period studied!!!!

In 1967, the editors of *Forbes* magazine also selected 28 stocks by throwing darts at a dart board. Their results also beat almost all of the professionally managed mutual funds!!!

William also found the *Wall Street Journal* ran a series of contests where professional managers tried to pick stocks that would out-perform stocks selected by using a dart board. Between 1990 and 1992, these contests at first showed the professional managers beating the dart board 24 times to 17 times. But, further analysis showed the dart board won if the results were discounted for two reasons.

The first reason was the fact the professionals selected stocks with much more risk than the dart board. If the level of risk was adjusted for, the professionals came out about even with the dart board. The second reason was that as soon as the professional's stock picks were published, the prices of those stocks went up because readers of the paper purchased them. If this effect was discounted for, the dart board picks beat the professional managers!!

DILBERT reprinted by permission of United Feature Syndicate, Inc.

Wilshire 5,000 and S&P 500 Studies

William decided to do some basic research of his own and see if the Efficient Market Theory was really correct. William reasoned that if a professionally managed common stock mutual fund can beat market indexes like the Wilshire 5,000 or S&P 500, he should be able to check and see if there were some mutual funds that really beat these two indexes every year.

William did some research on how many funds were able to beat the Wilshire 5,000. He made a chart of his findings:

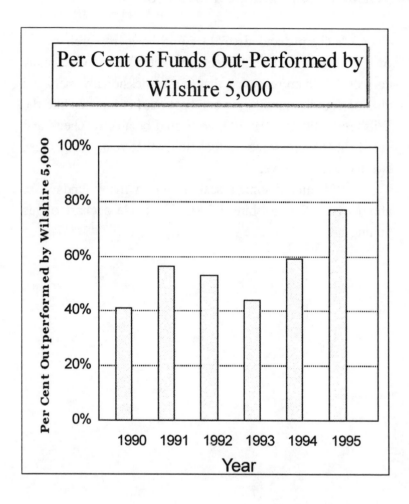

Per Cent of Funds Out-Performed by Wilshire 5,000

This chart showed William that from 1990 to 1995, anywhere from 41% to 77% of mutual funds were *unable* to equal the return of a benchmark such as the Wilshire 5,000!

William then researched to see how well managed funds fared against the S&P 500 market index. He found a study commissioned by the *Wall Street Journal* that found the S&P 500 outperformed 87% of mutual fund managers for the period 1969-1979. This study also found the S&P 500 outperformed 67% of mutual fund managers in the period 1972-1982. William found another study done by Lipper Analytical Services. The Lipper study found that the S&P 500 outperformed 88% of the common stock mutual funds over the period 1984 to 1988.

This series of studies demonstrated to William that a few mutual funds were able to beat market indexes like the Wilshire 5,000 or S&P 500 in any given year. William thought the real test would be to see if any professionally managed mutual fund could beat a market index every year, year after year.

Consumer Reports magazine tracked the performance of mutual funds compared to the S&P 500. William went to the library and got five consecutive years of *Consumer Reports* magazine. He made a table of the results he found:

Consistency of Performance of Mutual Funds

	1 year out of 5 years	2 years out of 5 years	3 years out of 5 years	4 years out of 5 years	5 years out of 5 years
Return more than 40% above 'S&P 500	43	2	0	0	0
Return 21-40% above S&P 500	29	3	0	0	0
Return ± 20% of S&P 500	69	49	33	8	0
Return 21-40% below S&P 500	115	56	14	2	0
Return more than 40% below S&P 500	60	61	59	42	24

William was shocked to discover that *no* mutual fund could beat the return of the S&P 500 every year five years in a row!! Furthermore, there were *no* professionally managed funds that came within ± 20% of the S&P 500 all five years!!

William was also surprised to discover how many consistently bad mutual funds there were!! There were 24 mutual funds that five years in a row returned more than 40% less than the S&P 500! William did not understand why an investor would leave money in funds that performed so badly. He guessed these investors did not know how to evaluate performance of mutual funds, or they were keeping them hoping they would give better performance someday.

An Index Fund is Born

William called Jill and told her he was ready to answer her question about why professional fund managers could not consistently beat the unmanaged market indexes. He gathered up his research papers and went to Jill's house.

William showed Jill all of his findings. He then summarized them for her:

- Professionally managed mutual funds have an inherent cost disadvantage compared to unmanaged indexes. Unmanaged indexes do not have to incur such costs as brokerage fees for buying and selling of stocks. The fund manager must charge each investor a per cent of their assets to cover these various costs. A professionally managed mutual fund will always have a 1% to 3% lower return to the investor than an unmanaged index.

- The U.S. stock market is studied by so many analysts and investors that it is an extremely efficient market. No individual mutual fund manager can outperform market indexes every year. This finding is supported by the following facts:

  - From 1990 to 1995, 41% to 77% of mutual funds were unable to beat the Wilshire 5,000 market index.
  - The S&P 500 outperformed 87% of mutual fund managers for the period 1969-1979.
  - The S&P 500 outperformed 67% of mutual fund managers for the period 1972-1982.

- The S&P 500 outperformed 88% of mutual fund managers for the period 1984-1988.
- Over a consecutive 5 year period, no mutual fund was able to beat the S&P 500 every year.
- Numerous studies have shown that monkeys throwing darts at a dart board with a list of stocks attached to it do a better job of picking stocks than professional money managers.

According to the fund industry, you should buy and hold a fund forever....the only way a fund gets paid is if you leave your money in their funds. The reality is that while they brainwash us into investment complacency, they furiously trade stocks like a Wild West gunslinger.

-- Tony Sagami of ProFutures, a money manager referral service in Austin, Texas.

- Professionally managed mutual funds also have an inherent tax disadvantage compared to a market index. Professional managers buy and sell stocks many times each year. The average turn-over ratio for mutual funds is 80%. This creates capital gain taxes which the mutual fund investors must pay. An index does no buying or selling except for the rare occasions when a company is added or removed from the index. Turn-over ratios of indexed funds can be as low as 2%. An index fund does have to invest new money, and may have to sell shares to pay investors who redeem shares from the fund.

Jill was astounded at William's findings. She asked William, "You mean I pay a professional mutual fund manager over a $100,000 a year to manage my portfolio, and I could tape the financial section of my newspaper to a dart board, throw darts at it, and probably have **better** results than the $100,000 a year manager??" William told her that she was correct.

Did you know the average age of a mutual fund portfolio manager is only 28 years old !!

Jill asked William if there was a mutual fund that simply mimicked one of the major market indexes. William told her that no such fund existed. Jill asked William why no one had ever started such a fund. William did not know why such a fund had never been created.

Jill and William discussed this for a while. Jill suddenly had a brainstorm idea. She suggested that William start a mutual fund indexed to a major market index like the S&P 500. William got very excited about Jill's idea. He began to furiously scribble some notes and formulas on a tablet. Jill then loaned William a calculator. After performing some calculations, William told Jill that a fund indexed to the S&P 500 could be designed so the annual fees to investors would be less than 0.2% a year!! This would be significantly less than the 1% to 3% charged by professionally managed funds. William told Jill that common stock mutual funds charge an average of 1.44% a year.

Jill asked William how he could physically create a mutual fund indexed to the S&P 500. William told her he would simply buy shares of all 500 companies that make up the S&P 500. He would also have to buy the same proportion of each company's shares just like the S&P 500 does. William told her his new index fund would give almost the same return as the S&P 500. His new fund would always give a little less return than the S&P 500 because of the expenses his fund had to incur.

William agreed to start a mutual fund indexed to the S&P 500. Jill suggested he name his new mutual fund "The S&P 500 Index Fund" since it was going to be indexed to the S&P 500 index.

Jill was one of the first investors in William's new index fund. As she got new money to invest, she put it into William's fund. She left her money in her nephew Ned's fund, but jokingly told him he needed to demonstrate he could beat the S&P 500 every year or she would transfer her money to William's new index fund!!!

Indexing Grows

Jill's and William's story above demonstrates why and how index common stock mutual funds were created. The very first common stock index mutual fund was created by Vanguard in 1976. In the Appendix, John Bogle describes the history and thoughts behind Vanguard's first index fund.

This fund took a while to get accepted by mutual fund investors. It took about 10 years to get over $1 Billion in assets according to the chart below:

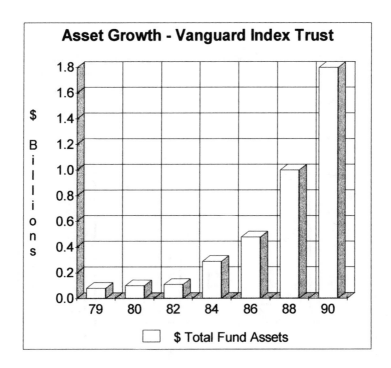

This fund then went through explosive growth in the 1990's as shown on the next page:

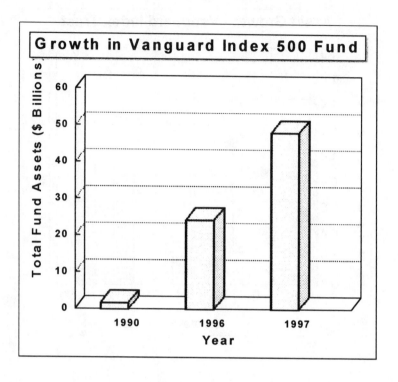

Growth in Vanguard Index 500 Fund

From the chart above, the assets invested in this fund exploded from $1.8 billion in 1990 to about $48 billion in 1997!!

Now there are so many different index funds available that newspapers and financial magazines often have a special section just for index funds!!

The Beardstown Ladies Controversy

The Beardstown Ladies were a group of gray-haired ladies in a small town in Illinois who formed their own stock investment club. They contributed money each month and used the money to buy and sell common stocks.

These ladies thought they were "beating the market" and published a book in 1994 about their investment success. The book claimed they achieved a 23.4% annual return on their common stock investments, which handily beat the Standard & Poor's 500 index return of 14.9% over this time period!!

The story of some small town gray-haired ladies picking stocks and beating the S&P 500 index was a classic Horatio Alger type "rags to riches" story. Their first book was extremely popular and sold over 800,000 copies. The ladies made all the television talk shows and developed their own cottage industry of book publishing and appearances.

In 1998, people began to question the accuracy of the 23.4% market beating returns the ladies achieved. The ladies had a prominent accounting firm check their calculations of their returns. It turned out the best estimate of the actual return the ladies achieved was more like 9%, *significantly less* than the 14.9% return of the S&P 500 !!!

This story helps to remind investors how difficult it is to consistently beat the returns of the stock market. If the ladies had invested in a mutual fund indexed to the S&P 500, they could have boosted their return from 9% to almost 15% !

Thing do not change, we do.
-Henry David Thoreau

DILBERT reprinted by permission of United Feature Syndicate, Inc.

Chapter 6

Index Fund Explosion

Since 1976 when Vanguard created the first indexed mutual fund, the number of indexed mutual funds available to investors has exploded. As of late 1997, there were at least 126 total index funds to choose from. There are several reasons why the number of available index funds has exploded.

Malkiel's Book

The number of index funds available probably increased due to a change in investor perceptions. Investor's perceptions about indexing as an investment strategy began to change in

1973 when Professor Burton Malkiel wrote the book *A Random Walk Down Wall Street.*

Professor Malkiel shocked the investment world by suggesting the stock market had become so efficient that no individual investor could consistently beat the returns of the over-all stock market. He argued that a mutual fund mimicking the over-all characteristics of the stock market could give better returns to investors that professional management of stock portfolios.

This book helped to educate investors about the use of indexed mutual funds. This book was probably the beginning of the change in investor's perception of indexed stock mutual funds.

Bogle's Influence

John Bogle has been Chairman of Vanguard mutual funds since 1974. Over the years, Bogle has been a tireless promoter of indexing. Not only did he promote the use of indexed mutual funds to Vanguard mutual fund investors, but his many public speeches and writings also reached countless other investors. An excerpt of one of Bogle's speeches on the development of index funds is included in the Appendix.

Bogle and Vanguard have been the leading pioneers of indexed mutual funds. Vanguard offered the first indexed common stock mutual fund in 1976. Vanguard has continued to be the leader in indexed funds by continuously introducing new funds indexed to various U.S. stock market indexes as well as to indexes of foreign stock markets.

In 1993, Bogle authored the book *Bogle on Mutual Funds*. This book promoted the use of indexed common stock mutual funds to investors.

Bogle's efforts to educate the investing public about the benefits of indexing have had a significant effect on investor's perception of indexing.

Personal Finance Magazines

In the mid-1990's, most of the personal finance magazines began to advocate the use of indexed common stock mutual funds. Many of these magazines began to recommend investors keep the bulk of their investments in common stock mutual funds indexed to either the S&P 500 or Wilshire 5,000.

Until the mid-1990's, the coverage of indexed mutual funds by personal finance magazines was rather sparse. As the evidence began to grow that indexed funds consistently beat the professionally managed funds, magazines began to recognize how important the indexing strategy was. The increase in the number of indexed mutual funds available and the large amount of money which flowed into them also prompted more coverage of indexing by the magazines.

In the August, 1995, issue of *Money* magazine, an editorial finally acknowledged that John Bogle was right and *"index funds rule"!* An excerpt of this editorial is included in the Appendix.

This increased coverage of indexing in the personal finance magazines helped to educate more investors and to change investor's perception of indexing.

The Internet

It is interesting to see how investor's perceptions of indexing have changed over the years. Before 1976, investors had never even heard of indexed mutual funds because they were not invented until 1976 by Vanguard.

Investors have become even more aware of indexing over the years due to the influence of Professor Malkiel, John Bogle, the Vanguard Group, and the personal finance magazines.

In the late 1990's, there are even Web sites devoted solely to indexing. One such Web site is Matthew Roberts' Web site at:

http://www.indexfundsonline.com/

Chapter 7

Why Haven't Index Funds Taken Over?

Using data available from the mutual fund industry, as of 1997, only about 4% of the money invested in common stock mutual funds was invested in indexed mutual funds!!

   If indexed stock funds consistently outperform professionally managed common stock funds, why don't indexed stock funds have more than 4% of the money invested in common stock mutual funds?

Indexed Stock Funds Not Available Until 1976

The first common stock indexed mutual fund was not available until 1976. If we assume most mutual fund investors start investing around age 30, this means investors older than 52 started out investing in non-indexed common stock funds.

According to U.S. Census data, investors over age 52 have about 80% of the net worth of all people in the United States. If these investors stayed with the same mutual funds they started with, probably 80% of the money invested in common stock funds was not invested in indexed funds.

The fact that indexed common stock mutual funds were not available until 1976 partially explains why index funds do not have the majority of funds invested in common stock mutual funds.

Lack of Education About Indexing

Most investors in mutual funds never had any formal education about investing either in high school or college. Most investors are not even aware of the concept of comparing the returns of a professionally managed mutual fund to an index which is indicative of the over-all stock market.

Once investors become aware they should compare their professionally managed fund's results to a market index like the S&P 500 or Wilshire 5,000, they start to question why their professionally managed fund is not doing as well as the market index.

Investors are not taught about mutual fund investing at their place of employment either. Many companies now offer 401(K) investment plans to their employees. Unfortunately, companies are very hesitant to recommend particular mutual funds to their employees for their 401(K) plans. Companies feel it is not their responsibility to teach employees about investment. Companies also feel they may face ill feelings or lawsuits from their employees if they recommend a mutual fund and it does not perform well.

Lack of education about mutual fund investing and indexing is one of the principal reasons index funds are not more popular.

No Financial Incentives to Sell Indexed Stock Funds

Stock brokers make their living from the commissions they receive from buying or selling investments to their customers. A stock broker will make a lot more money if he can convince his customers to buy and sell individual common stocks many times each year.

A stock broker makes much less money selling mutual funds to his customers. A stock broker will often "push" his customers to buy load versus no-load mutual funds. If the stock broker can convince his customer to buy a load type mutual fund, the stock broker gets a 5 to 8.5% commission from the sale. The broker receives most of this commission fee. The rest of the commission fee is paid to the mutual fund company.

A stock broker receives almost no compensation if he sells a no-load mutual fund to his customer. A no-load mutual fund is a fund the investor can buy directly from the mutual fund company without paying any commission. Since indexed stock funds are typically no-load type mutual funds, stock brokers have no financial incentive to recommend indexed mutual funds.

Financial planners also have no personal financial incentive to recommend indexed funds to their clients. The vast majority of financial planners are commission based planners versus fee-only type planners. Commission based planners earn their income by getting a commission each time they sell their client an investment. A typical example would be selling an investor an investment in a load type mutual fund. The planner gets to split a 7% commission with the mutual fund company. A fee-only planner charges for his services by the hour, and receives no commission for selling investments to his clients.

Since selling no-load index funds is the least lucrative method of increasing their income, brokers and financial planners do not promote indexed common stock mutual funds.

Mutual Fund Companies

Mutual fund companies typically make a lot more money selling professionally managed common stock mutual funds than selling indexed common stock funds.

Mutual fund companies make more money on professionally managed funds because they can charge the investors with management fees. These management fees not only compensate the fund for its expenses, but also provide a source of higher profits.

If a mutual fund company contemplates starting an indexed common stock fund, it must examine its competitors. Vanguard's Index 500 fund is the largest index fund. Vanguard's fund only charges investors about 0.2% a year in expenses.

For the new index fund to be successful, its expense ratio must be as low as Vanguard's 0.2%. A low expense ratio caps the profit level the new fund would achieve. The mutual fund company may decide it can make more profit on its existing professionally managed funds versus starting a new indexed fund.

The higher profits achieved by professionally managed funds may be a reason why more indexed funds are not created.

Indexed Stock Funds Not Available to 401(K) Investors

Many investors only invest in common stock mutual funds through their 401(K) plans at work.

Many companies hire a mutual fund or insurance company to administer their 401(K) plan. The mutual fund or insurance company often does not even have an indexed fund available to offer employees as part of the 401(K) plan.

Other mutual fund companies may have an indexed common stock fund, but they choose to not make it available to employees in their 401(K) plan.

401(K) plans usually offer a very limited number of common stock mutual funds for employees to invest in. Very seldom is an indexed fund included with the offerings for employees to choose from.

Lack of availability of index funds in 401(K) plans is another reason index funds are not more popular.

Indexing Not Exciting Enough

The concept of using indexed common stock mutual funds is so simple, that it is considered too boring by many people. Many investors receive personal pleasure from studying and trying to pick the hottest new mutual fund that just started up. They also may receive pleasure from selecting many different professionally managed funds and then determining which one does the best.

Indexing may not be exciting to some investors, but there are plenty of thrills to be had from watching your index fund beat the pros every single year!!

Indexing is about as glamorous as a box of rocks. -- From the book: Winning With Index Mutual Funds

---

Indexing Concept Hard to Believe

Psychologically, the concept of indexing can be hard to believe for many investors. After all, at first it seems tough to believe that a blind folded ape throwing darts at a dart board can achieve better results than a Harvard MBA getting paid more than $100,000 a year!!

Stock brokers also have trouble psychologically with indexing. They are trained by their parent company that better research on stocks will lead to better investment results. They are trained to convince their customers that their firm has the best research department on Wall Street, and therefore use of this research will yield better investment results.

I also initially had trouble believing in the concept of Efficient Markets and indexing. In the early 1990's, I conducted some exhaustive studies to try to find out if any professional mangers could beat the S&P 500 every year. I was shocked to find out that no professional managers could outperform the S&P 500 every year during the time periods I studied. These studies, plus the fact the S&P 500 has continued to beat the professional managers during the 1990's made a permanent believer out of me in the concept of indexing!!

Glorification of Professional Mutual Fund Managers

Successful professional mutual fund mangers are glorified in the media. Financial television programs offer exclusive interviews with successful managers. Personal finance magazines continuously run articles on the latest hot mutual fund manger. Financial newspapers also write about "*hot shot*" mutual fund mangers.

Many investors read or listen to this information and never think to compare the long term performance of the professional manager to a market index like the S&P 500 or Wilshire 5,000. Many of these investors would be shocked to learn the un-managed market indexes have beaten the best of these professional managers.

Failure of investors to compare the results of these glorified professional managers to market indexes has not helped the growth of indexed funds.

Bull Market

The Bull Market of the 1990's has blessed many investors with relatively high double digit returns.

Many investors are so pleased to receive double digit returns they do not even think about comparing their professionally managed fund's results to market indexes. They also don't worry about issues like high management fees and high taxes created by their professionally managed fund.

90

The Bull Market may indeed be another major reason why investors have not shifted from professionally managed funds to indexed funds.

Just Settling for Average Results

Many investors who know index funds exist, have the feeling that indexing is just settling for average results. They feel professional fund managers can and do beat the market averages.

Until these investors spend the time to learn that their professional fund managers can not consistently beat the market averages, they will probably continue to invest in professionally managed funds.

No Publicity from Personal Finance Magazines

Until the late 1990's, personal finance magazines basically ignored index funds. A 1995 editorial in *Money* magazine admitted they had ignored indexed funds. *Money* declared in this editorial that *"Index Funds Rule"!!*

See the Appendix for a copy
of this 1995 *Money* magazine
editorial.

This lack of publicity about indexed funds in the personal finance magazines also explains why index funds have not been more popular.

Chapter 8

Global Indexing

Let us return to the case of Jill, our fictitious investor. When we left Jill, she was contentedly investing in common stock index mutual funds. Jill's mutual funds were indexed to broad U.S. stock market indexes like the S&P 500 or Wilshire 5,000.

Although Jill was experiencing excellent returns on her indexed common stock mutual funds, she began to read more and more about exciting new markets in Europe and Asia. Some of the personal finance magazines she read were starting to recommend investing in these foreign markets.

Jill was doing well with her U.S. indexed investments, but wondered if she was missing out on some exciting foreign stock markets. She decided to call her old friend, William the Finance Professor, and set up a meeting with him.

Global Markets

When Jill called him, William was excited to hear from Jill. William had set up a very successful common stock index fund. There was a lot of initial work for William to keep him busy when he first set up the fund. Once the fund was set-up, it required almost no management from William because the fund only bought the common stocks in the index. William did not have to select stocks to buy and sell.

The fund was running very well with many satisfied investors, but William personally looked forward to new challenges. William was getting a little bored, so he looked forward to meeting with Jill.

Jill asked William about foreign stock investing. She expressed her concern about missing out on excellent opportunities in overseas markets.

William had also started to read about some of the exciting opportunities in overseas markets. William told Jill that he would do some research into the matter and then share his findings with her.

Overseas Investment Opportunities

William began to research investing overseas. His first step was to determine how large the overseas stock markets are compared to the U.S. stock market.

William found the U.S. stock market represents about 38% of the total world stock market. William made a pie chart to show this relationship:

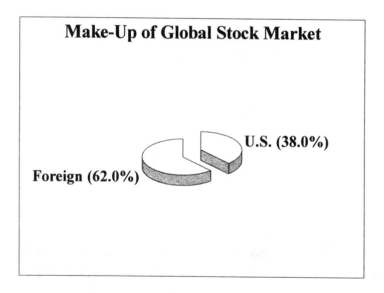

Make-Up of Global Stock Market

Foreign (62.0%)

U.S. (38.0%)

William was very surprised to find the United States represented *only one-third* of the world stock market!!

William then determined where all of the foreign stock market value was located. He found that half of the value was in the European stock market and half was in the Pacific stock market:

William charted this relationship also:

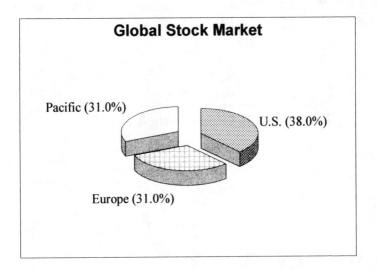

Global Stock Market

Pacific (31.0%)

U.S. (38.0%)

Europe (31.0%)

William knew the European stock market consisted of the major countries of Europe including England, France, and West Germany. William learned the Pacific stock market consisted of major Asian countries including Japan, Hong Kong, and Australia.

William did some further research and learned foreign stock markets often do not move up and down in value with the U.S. stock market. Since these foreign stock markets do not follow the U.S. market, investing in these foreign markets can help investors further diversify their portfolios. In some years, the U.S. stock market may go down while some foreign markets actually rise in value. This diversification effect allows investors to achieve higher returns with lower risk by investing in foreign stock markets as well as in the U.S. stock market.

William figured there was some bad news associated with foreign stock investment. He did some more research and learned there are four major areas of concern involved with investing in foreign stock markets.

The first area of concern he found was the general risk of the stock market itself. In any given foreign country, just like in the U.S., investors must deal with the risk of the markets going up and down in value.

The second area of concern with foreign stock investment is currency risk. Every day, the value of any foreign country's currency will change compared to the value of the U.S. dollar. It is possible that a particular foreign stock market will go up in value as expressed in terms of the local currency, but a U.S. investor might not benefit from investing in that foreign market. This could occur because the foreign currency changed in value with respect to the U.S. dollar such that the U.S. investor had no net gain in his investment.

The currency risk can be overcome by hedging foreign investments. Hedging involves paying a fee to guarantee a foreign currency will not change in value compared to the U.S. dollar. Because a fee must be paid to reduce this risk, the net return to the U.S. investor will suffer even if there is no change in exchange rates.

Political risk is a third risk foreign investors face. Many foreign countries do not have as stable a government as the United States. An assassination, revolution, or political scandal in a foreign country can adversely affect foreign investments.

The last area of concern of foreign investing is higher costs. It costs U.S. investors more money to participate in foreign stock markets. An investment in foreign stock markets will result in slightly lower returns than investing in U.S. markets due to higher costs.

A Foreign Index Fund is Born

William arranged a meeting with Jill to review his findings on foreign stock investment. He reviewed all the information he had discovered with Jill. Jill studied this information and thought about it for a while.

Jill told William it appeared to her investing in foreign stock markets had many advantages. A U.S. investor could further diversify a portfolio and achieve higher total returns by investing in foreign stock markets.

Jill asked William if she should invest 62% of her money in foreign stocks and 38% in U.S. stocks since this is how the global stock market is split up. William thought about Jill's question for a while. He then told Jill he did *not* think it was a good idea to invest such a high percentage of her assets in foreign stock markets. William reminded Jill of the higher risks of foreign investing from political risks and currency risks. William suggested that maybe 10 to 20% of her money should be invested in foreign stock markets.

Since Jill knew nothing about selecting individual common stocks in foreign countries, she asked William if there were mutual funds that invested in foreign stock markets. William told her there were many professionally managed funds that invested in foreign stock markets.

Because Jill had become such a believer in indexed mutual funds, she asked William if there were any mutual funds indexed to foreign stock markets. William told her there were no such funds.

Jill suggested to William that he start-up some new mutual funds indexed to foreign stock markets. After all, she reminded William, he had already started up a highly successful mutual fund indexed to the U.S. stock market.

William thought over Jill's suggestion for a few minutes. He told Jill he saw no reason he could not start up some new index funds. He thought he could start up several new funds. His first new fund could be indexed to the European stock market. His second new fund could be indexed to the Pacific stock markets. The third new fund could be indexed to the whole global stock market with 38% in the United States, 31% in Europe, and 31% in the Pacific!

Closing Thoughts

Jill's and William's story above demonstrates why and how indexed foreign stock mutual funds were created.

Some of the first indexed foreign stock mutual funds were created by Vanguard in 1990. One of these pioneering funds is the Vanguard International Equity Index Fund - European Portfolio which is indexed to the European stock market. The other pioneering fund is the Vanguard International Equity Index Fund - Pacific Portfolio which is indexed to the Pacific stock market.

By 1998, Vanguard's European indexed fund had grown to $2.43 billion and the Pacific fund to $827 million.

Mutual funds indexed to foreign stock markets remain very popular because they provide investors with some very valuable benefits. These benefits include:

- Investors can increase the diversification of their stock portfolio by investing in foreign stock markets. This increase in diversification can offer higher returns with lower risk versus investing just in the U.S. stock market.

- Investors can use indexing to assure they will achieve at least the same rate of return as the foreign stock market they are investing in. Investors do not have to rely on professional managers to pick stocks in foreign countries.

- Investors can use indexing to assure they are paying the lowest cost possible for the management of their mutual fund investments in foreign stock markets.

Chapter 9

Available Index Funds

Below is a list of some of the indexed common stock funds currently available to investors:

> *The number of index funds available grows every day. Check the financial section of your newspaper, there is probably a separate section just for index funds !!*

Fund Name	Index
ASM Index 30	Dow Jones Ind'ls
Vanguard Total Stock Mkt Index	Wilshire 5,000
Rydex OTC	Nasdaq 100
BT Inv Equity 500	S&P 500
Dreyfus S&P 500 Index	S&P 500
Fidelity Spartan Market Index	S&P 500
Galaxy II Large Company Index	S&P 500
Northern Stock Idx	S&P 500
Schwab S&P 500	S&P 500
SSgA S&P 500 Index Fund	S&P 500
Strong Index 500	S&P 500
T. Rowe Price Equity Index	S&P 500
Transamerica Premier Idx Inv	S&P 500
USAA S&P 500 Index	S&P 500
Vanguard 500 Portfolio	S&P 500
Schwab 1000	Schwab 1000
Dreyfus Midcap Index	S&P Midcap 400
Vanguard Extended Mkt Index	Wilshire 4500
Vanguard Small Cap Index	Russell 2000
Galaxy II Small Cap Index	S&P Small Cap 600
Vanguard Total Intntl	MSCI-EAFE
Vanguard European Index	MSCI Europe Index
Vanguard Pacific Index	MSCI Pacific Index
Vanguard Emerging Markets Indx	MSCI Emerging Mkt

As the previous chart demonstrates, mutual funds indexed to the S&P 500 are the most available type of index fund. Vanguard also obviously offers the largest selection of different types of indexed funds. Vanguard allows investors to use indexing to invest in foreign stock markets as well.

Since new index funds are being offered all the time, you should check and see if more funds are available that you can choose from. You can find the latest list of available index funds by checking the financial section of your newspaper under the index fund section, checking out a copy of one of the personal finance magazines such as *Money* magazine, or by using the Internet.

Check Index Fund Online's web site at
http:/www.IndexFundsOnLine.com
to see updated lists of available index
mutual funds

Since Vanguard has been the pioneer and leader of index funds, I would highly recommend you check out their mutual funds.

You can obtain a prospectus and application form for any of their index funds by called them at 800-662-2739 or contacting them at their web site at http://www.vanguard.com

Chapter 10

Selecting Common Stock Index Funds

Selecting the right common stock index funds depends on several factors.

U.S. Common Stock Index Funds

For that portion of your portfolio to be invested in U.S. stocks, you need to decide which index you want to follow. The broadest measure of the U.S. stock market is the Wilshire 5,000. This index covers almost 100% of the total value of U.S. stocks.

The Wilshire 5,000 is the broadest measure of the U.S. stock market you will find. You should select this index if you want your portfolio to mimic the whole U.S. stock market.

Mutual funds indexed to the S&P 500 are the most popular. They have the highest number of mutual funds to choose from. The S&P 500 is a popular index because it covers 500 large companies in the United States. The S&P 500 represents about 70% of the total value of U.S. stocks.

Since the S&P 500 primarily represents the largest companies in the United States, you will not be investing in the smaller companies in the United States. Many historical studies have shown smaller companies slightly outperform larger companies. If you choose the S&P 500, you will be investing in large, stable companies. You may miss some of the performance of the smaller companies.

I would suggest you choose a common stock mutual fund indexed to the Wilshire 5,000. I would recommend the Wilshire 5,000 index because it is the broadest measure of the U.S. stock market. It also includes both large and small companies. Buying a mutual fund indexed to the S&P 500 is acceptable as long as you understand you may be giving up some potentially greater returns from the smaller companies.

Foreign Common Stock Index Funds

For that portion of your portfolio to be invested in foreign stocks, you also need to decide which index you want to follow. Since roughly half of the foreign stock market's value is in Europe and half is in the Pacific, I would suggest you evenly split your foreign investments between Europe and the Pacific.

Vanguard offers mutual funds that allow you to invest in the whole foreign stock market, or separately in Europe and the Pacific. You should investigate their funds and choose the approach that best suits your needs.

You can obtain a prospectus and application form for any Vanguard foreign index fund by called them at 800-662-2739 or contacting them at their web site at http://www.vanguard.com

Japan

The Japanese stock market experienced one of the most severe stock market crashes of all time in 1989. The Japanese stock market lost about 50% of its value in this crash. I believe this crash was caused by too much government involvement in Japanese stocks and real estate.

The Japanese stock market has never recovered from this crash. In inflation adjusted terms, in 1998 the Japanese stock market is trading at less than 50% of its peak 1989 value.

Since the Japanese stock market has shown no signs of recovery for nine years, I would avoid indexed funds that invest in the Japanese stock market. I would suggest you find an indexed fund that invests in Asian markets, but does not invest in Japanese stocks.

Cost Considerations

When you pick which common stock index funds to invest in, you need to study the costs of each fund. All of the funds publish expense ratios which are a good yard stick to measure the cost efficiency of each fund. The lower the expense ratio, the lower the cost to you, which means net higher returns on your investments.

Traditionally, the Vanguard funds have been the cost efficiency leaders. Some of the Vanguard funds have expense ratios *less than 0.2%!!* You should compare the expense ratios of all the funds you investigate and choose the funds which have the lowest cost.

Other Considerations

There are many other considerations you should examine when selecting indexed common stock funds to invest in. Some of these considerations include:

- How long has the fund been in existence?

- How well has the fund tracked its index?

- What kind of customer service does the fund provide?

- Does the fund offer consolidated statements to reduce your paperwork if you own more than one fund in the same mutual fund family?

- Can the fund family offer you good indexed funds for both U.S. and foreign stock markets?

- How easy is it to redeem shares?

- Does the fund offer an automatic investment plan in which the fund automatically invests funds from your bank account each month?

John Bogle, founder of Vanguard mutual funds, has spoken out for years about mutual funds charging their customers too high of expense ratios. Check out the Vanguard Web site at www.vanguard.com to educate yourself more about mutual fund costs.

Chapter 11

Indexing Into Retirement

During most of the life of a typical investor, it makes sense to have almost all of your investments in common stocks. Although common stocks have the highest risk of any type of investment, they offer the highest potential returns as long as you are investing for five years or longer. Using indexed common stock funds is a very smart way to invest in common stocks.

Let's again look at Jill to see how she continues to use the concept of indexing as she prepares to enter the retirement stage of her life.

111

Getting Ready for Retirement

Jill used indexed common stock mutual funds to accumulate enough assets to support her during her retirement. Her indexed funds performed very well for her and she was on target for accumulating enough assets to retire. She estimated she would work for about five more years, then retire.

Lately, Jill has started to become nervous about her investments. She had been investing in indexed common stock mutual funds for about 20 years. Over those 20 years she had seen the stock market have some very good years. She had also seen the stock market have some very bad years. She had become nervous during those bad years, but she did not sell out because she knew time was on her side. Although there were some bad years, the stock market always came back and the value of her investments continued to grow.

With only five years to go until retirement, Jill did not want to take too much risk with the money she needed to live on during retirement. She also knew that if she withdrew from the stock market and put her money in the bank, she would be sure to lose money every year after inflation and taxes.

Jill decided to discuss this issue with her old friend William the Finance Professor.

Retirement Strategy

Jill met with William and reviewed her problem with him. William empathized with Jill because he was planning to retire in a couple of years also. He also had all of his financial assets invested in common stocks like Jill.

William told Jill they were looking at two options. In option number one, they could leave all of their money invested in common stocks. The advantage of this strategy was that over time, the stock market should let their financial assets continue to increase each year after inflation and taxes. The disadvantage of this strategy was the high risk of common stocks. This high risk could result in several bad years where the value of their stock portfolio was significantly reduced.

In option two, they could pull their money out of the stock market and put it all in the bank and collect interest. The advantage of this strategy was almost no risk of losing their investment. The disadvantage of this strategy was that every year they were guaranteed to lose money after inflation and taxes.

William told Jill there must be an option between these two choices where they accepted some risk and could stay ahead of inflation and taxes. William told Jill he would research this and get back to her with his findings.

Asset Allocation

William began to research this problem. He quickly discovered the principle of asset allocation. Asset allocation is where you divide your money among three different asset classes. These three asset classes are cash, bonds, and common stocks.

The cash portion of the portfolio is invested in safe investments that pay a defined interest rate. Examples of this include money market mutual funds and certificates of deposit.

The bond portion of the portfolio is invested in government or corporate bonds. A bond is an investment where the investor loans someone money. The borrower then repays the loan, plus interest, over a designated period of time. Bonds are riskier than cash type investments, but less risky than common stocks. Bonds also offer a higher rate of return than cash type investments, but not as high as common stocks.

Bonds are risky because their value changes with every change in interest rates. If interest rates go up, the value of your bond goes down. If interest rates go down, the value of your bond goes up. If you do not sell your bond until it matures, you will receive the rate of return you agreed to and get your principal back as well. If you must sell your bond before it matures, its value will depend on the interest rate at the time you sell your bond.

The last asset class in the allocation mix is common stocks. Although common stocks are the riskiest asset, they historically have been able to provide returns which exceed inflation and taxes.

After studying asset allocation theory further, William discovered that a blend of all three asset classes can give investors returns somewhere between cash and common stocks, with a total risk level also between cash and common stocks.

Asset Allocation and Investor's Age

William and Jill got back together and reviewed William's findings. After Jill thought about William's findings, she told William that asset allocation theory seemed to make sense.

Jill asked William how to determine the right blend of the three asset classes. William told her there is no secret formula such as 33% cash, 33% bonds, and 33% common stocks. William said that in the first half of the 20th century, many portfolio managers held 0% cash, 50% bonds, and 50% common stocks. He also told her that a 1950's rule of thumb was to subtract your age from 100 and keep that percent of your assets in common stocks. Under the 1950's rule of thumb, the portion of your assets not invested in common stocks should be invested in bonds.

William told Jill the blend should really match an investor's age and associated risk level. Someone just entering retirement needs to be sure their portfolio continues to grow in value after inflation and taxes. The portfolio needs to continue to grow so it can support the investor through the retirement years. The only way to assure growth is to favor the common stock portion of the blend. A typical blend for someone entering retirement might be 10% cash, 30% bonds, and 60% common stocks.

When the investor reaches the middle of his retirement period and wants to reduce the risk level of his portfolio, the blend needs to be adjusted. A typical blend for this investor might be 10% cash, 60% bonds, and 30% common stocks.

Using Indexing to Implement Asset Allocation

Jill decided that she wanted to start out with 10% cash, 30% bonds, and 60% common stocks as her blend for asset allocation. Since Jill liked the concept of indexing with her common stocks, she asked William if she could continue to use indexing for her asset allocation plan.

William told her she could continue to use indexed common stock mutual funds for the common stock portion of her portfolio.

Jill told William that she would like to continue to have 20% of her common stock money invested in foreign common stocks and 80% in U.S. common stocks. William told her she could continue to do this. William explained to Jill that 20% of her common stock portion of her asset allocation blend in foreign stocks meant that foreign stocks would be 12% of her total portfolio and U.S. stocks would be 48% of her total portfolio:

20% Foreign Stocks x 60% Common Stock

Allocation Blend = 12% of Total Portfolio

80% U.S. Stocks x 60% Common Stock

Allocation Blend = 48% of Total Portfolio

William told Jill that for the 10% cash portion of her portfolio, she could invest in money market mutual funds.

William then explained that for the 30% bond portion of her portfolio, she could choose an indexed bond fund. William told her that indexed bond funds are set-up the same way as indexed common stock mutual funds.

William then made two pie charts for Jill. The first one demonstrated her over-all asset allocation blend of 10% cash, 30% bonds, and 60% common stocks:

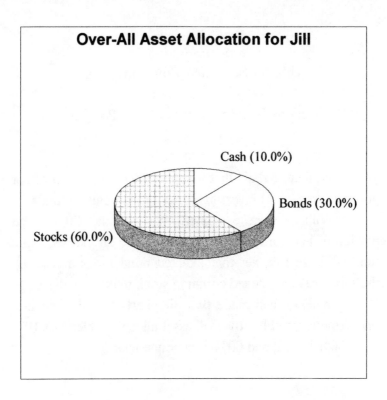

Over-All Asset Allocation for Jill

Cash (10.0%)

Bonds (30.0%)

Stocks (60.0%)

William then made a second pie chart to include Jill's plan to continue to invest in 20% indexed foreign stocks:

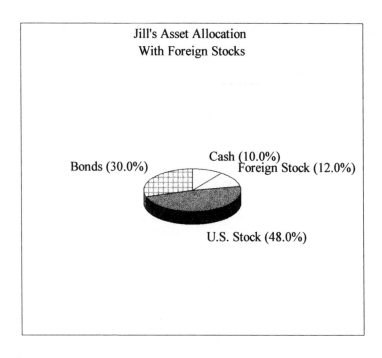

Jill's Asset Allocation
With Foreign Stocks

Bonds (30.0%)

Cash (10.0%)
Foreign Stock (12.0%)

U.S. Stock (48.0%)

After going through this exercise with William, Jill was now comfortable with the concept of asset allocation. She decided to select a money market mutual fund and an indexed bond mutual fund. Once she had the funds selected, she planned to start shifting her money around until she arrived at her 10% cash, 30% bonds, and 60% common stocks blend.

There is nothing permanent except change. --Heraclitus

Jill planned to monitor this allocation and adjust the blend over time as she got further along her retirement years. Jill also knew she would have to adjust the blend periodically due to changes caused by interest rate swings and stock market value changes.

Chapter 12

Still Think Your "Gunslinger" Can Beat the Market?

Adam Smith, in his book *The Money Game*, first published in 1967, popularized the term "gunslinger" for professional common stock mutual fund managers. He defined a gunslinger as a hot-shot professional fund manager who was able to beat the returns of the over-all stock market.

Many investors have difficulty accepting the fact highly educated and highly paid professional managers can *not* consistently beat the stock market. This chapter provides some "food for thought" for those investors who are still having trouble accepting the advantages of indexing.

Have You Compared the Professional's Performance to the Market's Averages?

If you think you have found a professional manager who can consistently beat the stock market, you need to compare the manager's performance to broad market averages.

I would suggest you compare your manager's performance to a broad market average like the S&P 500. Check and see if your manager has really demonstrated the ability to beat the S&P 500 every year. I will predict you will find that very few professional managers have beaten the S&P 500 every year!!

Also make sure your favorite professional manager is not taking much higher risks than the S&P 500 level of risk. General investment theory says the higher risk one takes, the higher the return can be. Unfortunately, the investor also has a higher chance of losing money as well!! Your professional manager should be able to beat the S&P 500 every year and not take higher risks than the S&P 500 portfolio of stocks.

The Professional Manager Faces a Heavy Cost Disadvantage

Your favorite professional manager has a very tough cost disadvantage to overcome compared to the returns generated by common stock index funds. The professional manager must charge you fees to cover his cost of buying and selling stocks many times each year.

Professionally managed funds turn over 80% of their stocks every year, while indexed funds only turn over about 2% of their stocks. Professionally managed funds charge an average expense ratio of 1.44% per year with some funds charging as high as 3%. An index fund does not have to incur these costs because it only buys the shares of the companies in the index. Vanguard's Index 500 fund only charges investors 0.2% per year!!

Make sure you compare the expense ratios of your professional's mutual fund to the relatively low expense ratios charged by the indexed funds. You will find your professional manager must out perform the S&P 500 by about 2% each year to end up matching the returns of the S&P 500 after expenses are considered!!

The Professional Manager Faces Tax Disadvantages Also

As an investor, you want to optimize your return after taxes. An index fund has a relatively low tax bite because it does not generate capital gains taxes from buying and selling different stocks all year.

If your favorite professional manager is successful and generates capital gains from buying and selling stocks in his portfolio, you will have to pay taxes on these gains.

Be sure and consider the tax consequences when you compare your professional manager's fund to an indexed fund. You will find that indexed funds have relatively good tax efficiencies for investors.

Very Few Professionals Have Consistently Beat the Market

There are very few professional managers who have beaten the stock market on a consistent basis. Those professional money managers who have beaten the market averages over long periods of time are very famous.

Some examples of present day investors who have demonstrated the ability to beat the market over long periods of time include Warren Buffet and Peter Lynch. Buffet runs Berkshire Hathaway and an investor can buy shares of his company. Unfortunately, Buffet is getting older and some say his Berkshire Hathaway shares are over valued.

Peter Lynch used to run Fidelity Magellan fund. Lynch demonstrated the ability to beat the market while he ran this fund. Lynch retired from managing specific funds and still acts as an investment advisor.

Is your favorite professional really as good as Buffet and Lynch?? The fact that only a few investors such as Buffet and Lynch have beaten the market consistently demonstrates how tough it is to beat the market!!

I like to buy a company any fool can manage,
because eventually one will. -- Peter Lynch,
former head of the Magellan fund
at Fidelity Investments.

Going Against The Advice of the Number One Personal Finance Magazine

In 1995, *Money* magazine finally came out for a new strategy of using common stock indexed funds as the core portion of an investment portfolio.

For many years, the personal finance magazines basically ignored indexed funds. They had a few stories about index funds, but their thrust was towards professionally managed funds.

Money acknowledged they had also ignored the index fund revolution, but the track record of index funds could no longer be ignored. *Money* suggested a new strategy of using indexed common stock mutual funds as the core or major portion of an investor's portfolio. *Money* suggested that for the non-indexed portion of the portfolio, investors could try to find professional managers that could beat the indexes.

So, are you smarter than the number one personal finance magazine in the United States? Do you still think your favorite professional manager can ***consistently*** beat the market averages?

I go to bed happy at night knowing that hair is growing on the faces of billions of males and on women's legs around the world while I sleep. It's more fun than counting sheep. -- Warren Buffett, whose Berkshire-Hathaway owns about 10% of The Gillette Company.

Compromise Strategy

If you still believe you can find professional managers that can beat the market averages, let me suggest a compromise strategy. Why not put 80% of your common stock investments into index funds that mimic broad market averages? Use the other 20% to try out those professional managers you think can beat the market.

You can monitor the annual performance of the professional managers. If the professional manager can consistently beat the market, you can give him more than 20% of your common stock portfolio to manage. If the professional manager can not beat the market averages year after year, you can try another professional manager, or simply put the money into the indexed funds.

Chapter 13

Activity Checklist

Indexing is a powerful tool you can use to help you meet your financial goals. The following list will help you use the power of indexing to meet your goals:

☑ Select a common stock index mutual fund to invest in.

☑ Open an account with the common stock index mutual fund you have selected.

☑ Read the index fund's reports and monitor your fund's progress.

☑ Subscribe to a personal finance magazine and learn more about indexing.

☑ Visit Vanguard's Web site and learn more about indexing at http://www.vanguard.com

☑ Investigate/participate in any employer sponsored savings plans (401(K), stock purchase plans, etc.). If you work in the non-profit or government sector, investigate/participate in 403(B) or 457 retirement plans. Use indexed common stock mutual funds if they are offered. If indexed funds are not offered, lobby your organization to get them added as an option.

☑ Investigate/participate in IRA's. Use indexed common stock mutual funds.

☑ Learn to use the Internet. Visit available Web sites to learn more about indexing.

☑ When you get within five years of retirement, start to develop and implement an asset allocation plan using indexed common stock and bond funds.

☑ Read some of the references in the Appendix.

Review your financial plan at least once a year. Make adjustments to your plan as needed to keep you on track to meet your goals.

Chapter 14

Summary

Index funds offer the chance for normal investors to beat the pros every year.

It is unfortunate that indexing has not caught on faster with the general population. If more investors had used indexing over the last 10 years, they would be *much* richer today!!

> *The Investment Company Institute maintains*
> *an interesting and educational Web site about*
> *mutual funds. Check it out at www.ICI.org*

There are some encouraging signs that index funds are beginning to gain rapidly in popularity. According to the Investment Company Institute, in 1995 about 6.9% of all the new money going into U.S. and international stock funds went into indexed stock mutual funds. In 1996, the amount of new money going into indexed stock mutual funds increased to 8.8% !!

Although I am confident indexing will continue to grow in popularity, it may take a major event to trigger the general public to become even more interested in indexing. Such a trigger may be the privatization of the Social Security program.

Imagine what would happen if investors were suddenly given the opportunity to be responsible for investing a portion or all of their Social Security funds. Suppose the government set up 10 different mutual funds for investors to choose from and one of those 10 was a common stock mutual fund indexed to the S&P 500. This event would definitely trigger a national dialogue on the merits of indexing versus professionally managed mutual funds!!

*The United States would **not** be the first country to privatize its Social Security system. Chile, England, and Mexico already have a privatized Social Security system !!*

Another factor which may drive more investors to index funds is the stock market returning to more "normal" advances each year. With a 30% return a year, the 2% penalty of higher costs of professionally managed funds versus index funds does not seem to be a big factor to most investors.

When 10% a year stock market advances do occur again, the 2% penalty of professionally managed funds will represent a loss of 20% of the net return an investor receives. A slow down in the annual growth of the stock market may trigger more interest in index funds because cost penalties will become more significant.

It is hoped this book has provided you with an understanding of the basic concepts of indexing so you can use indexing to help achieve your financial goals.

Once you are comfortable and experienced with the concepts of indexing covered in this book, I encourage you to learn more about indexing and investment using some of the reference materials shown in the Appendix.

> *If you come up with a financial plan, odds are you **will** achieve 80% of your goal even if you barely try. If you have no plan, you will probably **never** achieve your goals.*

Appendix

This is an excerpt from a speech given by John Bogle on how index funds were first conceived:

The Beginning

Here is what happened and how it happened.*

I suppose the beginning of the first index mutual fund goes back to 1949. When I was a junior at Princeton University looking for an idea for my senior thesis, I sought a topic that literally no one had ever written about in a serious academic paper. I stumbled upon an article in *Fortune* magazine (December 1949) entitled "Big Money in Boston." It was the first time I had ever thought about the mutual fund industry. When I read that "mutual funds may look like pretty small change," but constituted a "rapidly expanding and somewhat contentious industry" that could be of "great potential significance to U.S. business," I knew I had found my topic.

After a year-and-a-half of research and writing this thesis, prepared by a callow and idealistic young scholarship student working his way through a great University, I concluded with several main themes, including suggesting that the industry's future growth could be maximized by a "reduction of sales loads and management fees"; that "fund investment objectives must be stated explicitly"; that mutual funds should avoid creating "the expectations of miracles fund management"; and (based on the evidence I had ascertained) should "make no claim for superiority over the market averages." Others have interpreted these thoughts as a precursor of my later interest in matching the market with an index fund. Honestly, I don't know whether they were or not. Today, nonetheless, if I had to name the moment when the seed was planted that germinated into the presentation of the first index mutual fund to the Vanguard Board in 1975, that would be it.

The basic ideas go back a few years earlier. In 1969–1971, Wells Fargo Bank had worked from academic models to develop the principles and techniques leading to index investing. John A. McQuown and William L. Fouse pioneered the effort, which led to the construction of a $6 million index account for the pension fund of Samsonite Corporation.

With a strategy based on an equal-weighted index of New York Stock Exchange equities, its execution was described as "a nightmare." The strategy was abandoned in 1976, replaced with a market-weighted strategy using the Standard & Poor's 500 Composite Stock Price Index. The first such models were accounts run by Wells Fargo for its own pension fund and for Illinois Bell.

In 1971, Batterymarch Financial Management of Boston independently decided to pursue the idea of index investing. The developers were Jeremy Grantham and Dean LeBaron, two of the founders of the firm. Grantham described the idea at a Harvard Business School seminar in 1971, but found no takers until 1973. For its efforts, Batterymarch won the prize for the "Dubious Achievement Award" from *Pensions & Investments* magazine in 1972.**

It was two years later, in December 1974, when the firm finally attracted its first client. By the time American National Bank in Chicago created a common trust fund modeled on the S&P 500 Index in 1974 (requiring a minimum investment of $100,000), the idea had begun to spread from academia—and these three firms that were the first professional believers—to a public forum.

Gradually, the press began to comment on index investing. A cri de coeur calling for index funds to be formed came from each of several intelligent and farsighted observers.*** I still have those articles that I read nearly 23 years ago; they read just as well today.

The first article was "Challenge to Judgment," by Paul A. Samuelson, Professor of Finance at Massachusetts Institute of Technology. In *The Journal of Portfolio Management* (Fall 1974), he pleaded "that, at the least, some large foundation set up an in-house portfolio that tracks the S&P 500 Index—if only for the purpose of setting up a naive model against which their in-house gunslingers can measure their prowess. . . .Perhaps CREF (College Retirement Equities Fund) can be induced to set up a pilot-plant operation of an unmanaged diversified fund, but I would not bet on it. . . . The American Economic Association might contemplate setting up for its members a no-load, no-management-fee, virtually no-transaction-turnover fund" (noting, however, the perhaps insurmountable difficulty that "there may be less supernumerary wealth to be found among 20,000 economists than among 20,000 chiropractors").

Dr. Samuelson concluded his "challenge to judgment" by explicitly calling for those who disagreed that a passive index would outperform most active managers to dispose of "that uncomfortable brute fact (that it is virtually impossible for academics with access to public records to identify any consistently excellent performers) in the only way that any fact is disposed of—by producing brute evidence to the contrary." There is no record that anyone tried to produce such brute evidence, nor is it likely that it could have been produced. But Dr. Samuelson had laid down an implicit challenge for somebody, somewhere to start an index fund.

A year later, Charles D. Ellis, President of Greenwich Associates, wrote a seminal article entitled "The Loser's Game" in *The Financial Analysts Journal* for July/August 1975. Ellis quickly offered a provocative and bold statement: "The investment management business is built upon a simple and basic belief: Professional managers can beat the market. That premise appears to be false." He pointed out that over the prior decade, 85% of institutional investors had underperformed the return of the S&P 500 Index, largely because "money management has become a Loser's Game. . . . Institutional investors have become, and will continue to be, the dominant feature of their own environment . . . causing the transformation that took money management from a Winner's Game to a Loser's Game. The ultimate outcome is determined by who can lose the fewest points, not who can win them." He went on to note that "gambling in a casino where the house takes 20% of every pot is obviously a Loser's Game."

Finally, Ellis went to the underlying economics of the matter: If equities provide an average return of 9% a year, and a manager generates 30% portfolio turnover at a cost of 3% of the principal value on both the sales and the reinvestment of the proceeds (a reduction in return equal to 1.8% of assets per year) and charges management and custody fees equal to 0.2% (low!), the active manager incurs costs of 2%. Therefore, he must achieve an annual return of +11% before these costs—that is, 22% above the market's return—just to equal the gross market return. (That 2% aggregate cost remains pretty much the same—although of a somewhat different composition —for mutual funds in 1997, 22 years later.) While Ellis did not call for the formation of an index fund, he did ask: "Does the index necessarily lead to an entirely passive index portfolio?" He answered, "No, it doesn't necessarily lead in that direction. Not quite. But if you can't beat the market, you should certainly consider joining it. An index fund is one way." In the real world, of course, few managers indeed have consistently been able to add more than those two percentage points of annual return necessary merely to match the index, and even those few have been exceptionally difficult to identify in advance.

The third article, by Associate Editor A.F. Ehrbar, appeared in *Fortune*, the magazine that in 1949 had provided me with my original inspiration to write about mutual funds. In July 1975, in an article entitled "Some Kinds of Mutual Funds Make Sense," Ehrbar concluded some things that seem pretty obvious today: "While funds cannot consistently outperform the market, they can consistently underperform it by generating excessive research costs (i.e., management fees) and trading costs. . . . It is clear that prospective buyers of mutual funds should look over the costs before making any decisions." He concluded that "funds actually do worse than the market." He had little hope that the mutual fund industry would rush to fill the gap created by the new view that cost is the principal reason that investors as a group are unable to outpace the market index.

Ehrbar despaired about the remote likelihood that an index mutual fund would be created very soon, noting that "there has not been much pioneering lately. While the mutual-fund industry has not provided an index fund, the American Bank of Chicago has put together a common trust fund that aims to match the performance of the S&P 500 Index." (He failed to note that, with an annual fee of 0.8%, it could not possibly do so.) But he described the best alternative for mutual fund investors: "a no-load mutual fund with low expenses and management fees, about the same degree of risk as the market as a whole, and a policy of always being fully invested." He could not have realized that he had described, with some considerable accuracy, the first index mutual fund, soon to be formed. But that is exactly what he had done.

Confronted with those three articles, I couldn't stand it any longer. It now seemed clear that the newly formed Vanguard Group (then only a few months old) ought to be "in the vanguard" of this new logical concept, so strongly supported by data on past fund performance, so well known in academia but acknowledged by few in the industry. It was the opportunity of a lifetime: to at once prove that the basic principles enunciated in the articles could be put into practice and work effectively, and to mark this upstart of a firm as a pioneer in a new wave of industry development. With luck and hard work, the idea that began to germinate in my mind in 1949 could finally become a reality.

*Based on my Princeton senior thesis, presentations to the Vanguard Board of Directors, extensive notes taken as the events occurred, 22 consecutive Chairman's Letters in Vanguard Index Trust Annual Reports, and my speeches over the same period.

**A fine history of the Wells Fargo effort is presented in Peter Bernstein's Capital Ideas (Macmillan, Inc., 1992). The Batterymarch story is told in *Program Trading* (J.K. Lasser Institute, 1987), by Jeffrey D. Miller.

***I should note that one of the earliest calls
for indexing came from a book that I did
not read until some years later: *A
Random Walk Down Wall Street*, by
Princeton University Professor Burton
S. Malkiel (W.W. Norton, 1973). Dr.
Malkiel suggested "A New Investment
Instrument: a no-load, minimum-
management-fee mutual fund that
simply buys the hundreds of stocks
making up the market averages and
does no trading (of securities). . . . Fund
spokesmen are quick to point out, 'you
can't buy the averages.' It's about time
the public could." He urged that the
New York Stock Exchange sponsor such
a fund and run it on a nonprofit basis,
but if it "is unwilling to do it, I hope
some other institution will." In 1977,
four years after he wrote those words, he
joined the Board of Directors of First
Index Investment Trust and the other
Vanguard funds, positions in which he
has served with distinction to this day.

This speech reprinted with permission from John C. Bogle - Senior Chairman of the Vanguard Group.

Appendix

This editorial by Tyler Mathisen appeared in the August, 1995, edition of *Money* magazine. This change in direction regarding index funds by the largest personal finance magazine symbolized the emergence of index fund investment into the mainstream!

Bogle wins: Index funds rule

For nearly two decades, John Bogle, the tart-tongued chairman of the $155 billion Vanguard Group, has preached the virtues of index funds — those boring portfolios that aim to match the performance of a market barometer. And for much of that time, millions of fund investors (not to mention dozens of financial journalists including this one) basically ignored him.

Sure, we recognized the intrinsic merits of index funds, such as low annual expenses and, because the funds keep turnover to a minimum, tiny transaction costs. Moreover, because index fund managers convert paper profits into realized gains less frequently than do the skippers of actively managed funds, shareholders pay less tax each year to Uncle Sam. To be sure, those three advantages form a trio as impressive as Domingo, Pavarotti and Carreras.

And yet there was always this nagging conceptual obstacle that kept many investors from embracing the funds that Jack Bogle has pitched so vigorously for Vanguard: When you invest in an index fund, you're settling for average. Or so the thinking goes. For most fund investors, myself included (in fact, I own some actively managed Vanguard funds), the prospect of merely matching the market was simply not good enough.

Well, Jack, we were wrong. Now, just as you prepare at age 66 to step down as Vanguard CEO early next year, we're ready to say it: You win. Settling for average is good enough, at least for a substantial portion of most investors' stock and bond portfolios. In fact, more often than not, aiming for benchmark-matching returns through index funds assures shareholders of a better-than-average chance of outperforming the typical managed stock or bond portfolio. It's the paradox of fund investing today: Gunning for average is your best shot at finishing above average.

Want proof? Then check out the dramatic table that illustrates this month's story by associate editor Walter L. Updegrave, *"Why Funds Don't Do Better"* . It shows that in any given year during the past 20 years, as well as over longer periods within that span, your odds of besting the S&P 500-stock index in a diversified equity fund have been depressingly slim. Indeed, only three times in the past dozen years through 1994 have more than 50% of diversified equity funds outpaced the S&P.

"People don't realize how good indexing is," Bogle recently told Updegrave. "Matching the market or almost matching it is not a confession of failure." Far from it, considering that the S&P 500 index topped 83% of all general equity funds over the past decade.

So why can't more funds beat the market? And more important, in light of these chilling figures, what should you do now?

The answers to those questions and more are at the heart of this special report on mutual funds. Taken together, Updegrave's trenchant discussion of why funds usually underperform the indexes, plus staff writer Carla Fried's "*The New Way to Make More Money in Funds*" call for nothing less than a complete reorientation of your expectations as a fund investor. What's more, they guide you through a thorough, sophisticated rethinking of how to assemble a winning mutual fund portfolio.

No, we don't think it ought to consist entirely of index funds. As even Bogle admits, some managers have demonstrated an ability to outrun the markets over long periods. "There's no question," he says, "that some people are going to do better." And in foreign markets and selected domestic sectors, such as small-company shares, we believe that certain top stock pickers, whose funds Fried names, can add value.

To subscribe to Money, buy a copy at your local book store and send in the subscription card!!

All in all, though, we've come around to agreeing with the sometimes prickly, always provocative, fund exec known to admirers and detractors alike as Saint Jack: Indexing should form the core of most investors' fund portfolios. So here's to you, Jack. You have a right to call it, as you recently did in a Vanguard sales booklet you wrote, *"The Triumph of Indexing."*

Appendix

Compound Interest Formula

For those of you who know a little math and want to know precisely how to calculate compound interest, the formula for compound interest is:

$$FV = PV \times (1 + i)^n$$

Where: FV = Future value of investment

      PV = Present value of investment

      i = interest rate or rate of return on your investment

      n = number of years

Now, let's do an example problem:

- You want to invest for 10 years
- You will invest $100
- You will get a 10% rate of return
- How much will the investment be worth in 10 years?

PV = $100
i   = 0.10   (which is same as 10%)
n   = 10 years
FV = ??

$$FV = 100 \times (1 + 0.10)^{10}$$

$$FV = \$259.37$$

So, your $100 will grow to $259.37 in 10 years if you achieve a 10% rate of return.

The most fascinating results occur when you look at how much your money can grow over long periods of time.

- You want to invest for 40 years
- You will invest $10,000
- You will get a 10% rate of return
- How much will the investment be worth in 40 years?

PV   = $10,000
i   =   0.10   (which is same as 10%)
n   =   40 years
FV   =   ??

$$FV = 10,000 \times (1 + 0.10)^{40}$$

FV = $452,593

So, your $10,000 will grow to $452,593 in 40 years if you achieve a 10% rate of return !!

By applying some algebra, you can manipulate the compound interest formula above to solve for any of the four variables involved with compound interest.

Other Investment Resources

401(K)

Getting the Most Out of Your 401(K). A June 1996 *Your Money* magazine article explaining the basics of 401(K) accounts.

The Baby Boomers

The Pig and the Python: How to Prosper from the Aging Baby Boom by David Cork and Susan Lightsone. A very interesting book which helps to explain how the 76 million Boomers have affected society and how they may impact the stock market.

The Beardstown Ladies

The Beardstown Ladies Common Sense Investment Guide: How We Beat The Stock Market - And How You Can Too by The Beardstown Ladies Investment Club. The original book of how a group of gray-haired ladies in Illinois were able to achieve returns higher than the S&P 500.

But Their Recipes Were Great by Black/Toby. A May 1998 *Kiplinger's Personal Finance* magazine article describing that the Beardstown ladies really did not beat the S&P 500.

Financial Planners

Institute of Certified Financial Planners. Financial planners approved by the Certified Financial Planner Board of Standards, a professional regulatory body, 800-282-7526.

International Association for Financial Planning. To find financial planners in your area call 800-945-4237.

Money Managers Are Everywhere by Ken Sheets. A February 1995 *Kiplinger Personal Finance* magazine article on how to select a financial advisor.

National Association of Personal Financial Advisors. To find fee-only planners call 888-333-6659.

Smart Ways to Find a Financial Planner by Laura Koss-Feder. A March 1997 *Money* magazine article detailing how to find a good financial planner.

The Truth About Financial Planners by John Rubino. A December 1995 *Your Money* magazine article describing how to choose a financial planner.

Financial Planning Software

Build Up Your Retirement Savings with this Crystal-Clear Strategy by Eric Tyson. A March 1997 *Money* magazine article describing financial planning software and recommended values for future values of inflation, returns, tax rate, and life expectancy.

Financial Scams

Hustlers and Con Men by Jay Robert Nash. An excellent book describing many different financial scams carried out through the years.

With Friends Like These by John Anderson. A November 1996 *Smart Money* magazine article describing one modern day con man.

General Economics

Economics in One Lesson by Henry Hazlitt. Probably the simplest and best book ever written about understanding basic economics. Includes excellent examples of the real effects of government policies on the economy, business, citizens, and investors. A must read for investors because a basic understanding of economics is required to become a successful investor. Should be required reading in high school for every American.

How To Understand Economics in 1 Hour by Marshall Payn. Another easy method of learning basic economics.

General Financial Planning

The Complete Financial Guide to the 1990's by Gary L. Klott. Good general financial planning reference.

The Craft of Investing by John Train. General planning information including stock investing, retirement, and estate planning.

Kiplinger's Personal Finance Magazine. Similar in content to *Money*, but offers additional types of advice.

Money Dynamics for the 1990's by Venita VanCaspel. Very good reference for all areas of investment.

Money magazine. Continuously publishes investment articles and financial planning advice.

Smart Money magazine. Another magazine similar to Money and Kiplinger's.

The Wall Street Journal. Often has special articles on latest trends in investment including changes in tax law.

The Wealthy Barber: Everyone's Commonsense Guide to Becoming Financially Independent by David Chilton. Covers general basics of financial planning.

How to Become a Millionaire

The Millionaire Next Door: The Surprising Secrets of America's Wealthy by William D. Danko and Thomas J Stanley. Although many of the findings about millionaires should be common sense to most investors, these two authors review their findings about millionaires and validate how common sense is used by millionaires. They use their findings to teach how investors can become millionaires. Good book for investors who want to accumulate wealth to meet their long term financial goals. Makes one realize that if you want to accumulate a lot of wealth, you must be prepared to live below your means for many years. If you live below your means, you can save and grow the savings into real wealth. If it is more important to you to immediately consume all your earnings, you can not accumulate significant wealth. If you enjoy saving money by buying used vehicles, you will love the habits of millionaires who buy vehicles by the pound!! You can also use the author's simple net worth formula to see what kind of wealth accumulator you are. Investors should read this book so they have a clear understanding of the trade-offs between short term consumption versus long term wealth accumulation.

Index Funds

Are You Buying the Wrong Index? by Robert Barker. December 1996 *Smart Money* magazine article revealing that Burton Malkiel has now revised his recommendation of buying index funds which mimic the S&P 500. Malkiel now argues that so many investors adopted his recommendation that the S&P 500 is now overvalued. Malkiel now advocates investing in index which mimic broader indexes such as the Wilshire 5000.

The Feeling Isn't Mutual by David and Tom Gardner. A November 1996 *Smart Money* magazine article outlining why index funds are better than professionally managed common stock mutual funds.

Making Money Mirroring the Market by Penelope Wang. A January 1997 *Money* magazine article listing all index funds currently available.

How You Can Climb with Index Funds by Steven Goldberg. A March 1998 *Kiplinger's Personal Finance* magazine article on using index funds to achieve your short and long term goals.

How to Beat 77% of Fund Investors Year After Year by Jason Zweig. An August 1997 *Money* magazine article reviewing how index funds have beaten the performance of professional fund managers.

Make Money Mirroring the Market by Penelope Wang. A January 1997 *Money* magazine article reviews the explosion in the number of index funds available.

The New Tax Law...Mutual Funds to Buy Now by Alan Lavine. A March 1998 *Your Money* magazine article explaining why indexed funds have the best tax efficiency for investors.

The New Way to Make Money in Funds by Carla Fried and Jerry Edgerton. An August 1995 *Money* magazine article which documents Money magazine changing its investment recommendation to indexing. They recommend that investors put 45% to 70% of their money in common stock index funds. The balance of the money can be invested with professional managers who have shown they can beat the market averages.

A Random Walk Down Wall Street by Burton G. Malkiel.
Malkiel is a proponent of efficient market theory which says no mutual fund manager can consistently beat the stock market. Advocates investors using index funds instead of trying to find a portfolio manager who can beat the market.

Winning with Index Mutual Funds: How to Beat Wall Street at its own game by Jerry Tweddell and Jack Pierce.
Explains index fund investment.

Insurance

The 30-Minute Life Insurance Workout by Ronaleen Roha.
A June 1996 *Kiplinger Personal Finance* magazine article outlining how to calculate what amount of life insurance you need rather than relying on the 5 to 7 times salary rule of thumb.

The Best Way to Protect Yourself and Your Assets Against a Lawsuit by Amanda Walmac. An August 1996 *Money* magazine article with a very good explanation of umbrella policies.

How to Get Your Money's Worth in Home and Auto Insurance by Barbara Taylor. Sponsored by the Insurance Information Institute, a good review of home and auto insurance.

Personal Finance, An Integrated Planning Approach by Bernard Winger and Ralph Frasca. Introductory college level textbook with good explanation of all forms of insurance.

Stacking the Deck by Walter Updegrave. An August 1996 *Money* magazine article criticizing some of the practices of the insurance industry.

Investor Psychology

Extraordinary Popular Delusions & the Madness of Crowds by Charles MacKay and Andrew Tobias. Most investors who have been investing in stocks for many years agree the stock market is a combination of financial information and investor psychology. Stock market investors often behave like a crowd, especially in market crashes and roaring bull markets. Although written back in 1841, the first 101 pages offer one of the best historical reviews of the behavior of crowds of investors. The stories of the Mississippi Scheme, the South-Sea Bubble, and Tulipomania continue to help educate today's investors on crowd behavior. Every investor should read the first 101 pages so they can "weather the storm" the next time there is a market crash.

Mutual Funds

The 7 Deadly Sins of Investing by Robert Frick. A March 1998 *Kiplinger's Personal Finance* magazine article which tries to explain why investors leave money in poorly performing mutual funds.

12 Deadly Fund Myths and How to Profit from Them by Jason Zweig. A February 1996 *Money* magazine article which debunks common myths about mutual funds.

Bogle on Mutual Funds: New Perspectives for the Intelligent Investor by John C. Bogle. One of the best books ever written about mutual funds and index funds. Bogle has been a tireless promoter of index funds for years. He helped Vanguard become the world leader in index funds. He does an excellent job of explaining mutual funds and why index funds should be the core holdings of most investors. A must read for every mutual fund and index fund investor.

How Funds Can Do Better by Jason Zweig. A February 1998 *Money* magazine article reviewing 10 problems that mutual fund companies need to improve on.

The Money Game by Adam Smith. One would think a book originally published in 1967 would no longer be relevant to today's stock market. Quite the opposite is true. Adam Smith's observations about the stock market could be taken from today's headlines. His discussions about company earnings, manipulation of those earnings, and Wall Street's reaction to missed earnings targets are replayed every day on Wall Street. His observations about the deification of successful mutual fund managers is repeated today on television and personal finance magazines. His stories about picking high tech names for companies so their stock will sell better on Wall Street is also repeated today. Smith's insights have helped numerous investors get a good understanding of Wall Street, the stock market, mutual funds, and mutual fund managers.

No-Nonsense Guide to Understanding Mutual Funds by Arnold Corrigan and Phyllis Kaufman. Easy to read explanation of stock mutual funds.

Selection of Common Stocks

44 Years of History Say Buy These Stocks Now by Susan Scherreik. A *Money* magazine article reviewing and applying the price to sales ratio method of selecting common stocks.

Buffet - The Making of an American Capitalist by Roger Lowenstein. A review of one of the greatest investors of all times.

The Foolish Four by Tom and David Gardner. A February 1996 *Smart Money* magazine article describing the stock selection method of picking the four highest yield Dow 30 stocks each year.

Go Forth and Multiply. A December 1996 *Smart Money* magazine article describing 5 methods of common stock selection.

The Intelligent Investor by Benjamin Graham. Easier to read than Graham and Dodd's Security Analysis, and therefore more appropriate reading for most investors.

Martin Zweig's Winning on Wall Street by Martin Zweig. Martin Zweig is a successful investor and he reviews his method for selecting common stocks.

The Money Masters by John Train. Train studies the great investors including Warren Buffett, Paul Cabot, Philip Fisher, Benjamin Graham, T. Rowe Price, John Templeton, Larry Tisch, and Robert Wilson.

The New Money Masters by John Train. Train continues to study great investors including Jim Rogers, Philip Carret, George Soros, John Neff, and Peter Lynch.

One Up on Wall Street by Peter Lynch. Lynch was a mutual fund portfolio manager who produced some of the highest returns of any portfolio manager.

The Secrets of "Big Mo" Investing by Manuel Schiffres. A February 1996 *Money* magazine article describing how a mutual fund tries to apply the theory of momentum investing.

Security Analysis by Benjamin Graham and David Dodd. The earliest and most comprehensive review of how to evaluate common stocks.

A Supposedly Foolproof Way to Make Money In Stocks by Manual Schiffres. A March 1996 *Kiplinger's Personal Finance* magazine article describing the stock selection method of picking the 10 highest yield Dow 30 stocks each year.

What Has Worked in Investing - Studies of Investment Approaches and Characteristics Associated with Exceptional Returns by Tweedy, Browne Company. A collection of 44 studies which substantiate the value style of investing including global stock markets.

What Works on Wall Street by James O'Shaughnessy. Pioneering research on the price to sales ratio method of selecting common stocks.

The Social Security System

An Aging Population: Opposing Viewpoints by Charles Cozic. A series of articles arguing for saving the Social Security system, abolishing it, or privatizing it.

Baby Boomers by Paul Light. Discussion of whole range of Baby Boomer issues including the impact on the Social Security system.

The Case for Killing Social Security by George Church and Richard Lacayo. A March 1995 *Time* magazine article describing some of the problems with the Social Security system.

Empowering Workers: The Privatization of Social Security in Chile by Jose Pinera. A Cato Institute essay describing the 15 year privatized system in Chile.

How We Privatized Social Security in Chile by Jose Pinera. An interesting article in the July 1997 edition of *The Freeman* magazine describing how privatized Social Security was phased in.

The Stock Market

Investment: Concepts, Analysis, and Strategy by Robert Radcliffe. College level textbook covering all areas of investment including diversification.

Money Guide. The Stock Market by Money magazine. General primer on the workings of the stock market.

Understanding Wall Street by Jeffrey Little and Lucien Rhodes. Another good primer on the stock market.

Understanding Financial Statements by The New York Stock Exchange. A basic review of accounting and company financial statements.

Stock Brokers

Liar's Poker by Michael Lewis. Inside look at how stock brokers are trained and how they operate.

What Your Stock Broker Doesn't Want You to Know by Bruce Sankin. Describes some stock brokerage practices.

Targeting a Top Money Manager by Walter Updegrave. A February 1992 *Money* magazine article describing how to pick a stock broker.

Tax Software

Ten Things Your Tax Software Won't Tell You by Clifton Leaf. A March 1997 *Smart Money* magazine article reviewing the pros and cons of using tax preparation software.

Glossary of Investment Terms

401(K): A U.S. Government program where some workers can defer taxes on personal investments.

Allocation mutual fund: A mutual fund that allocates its investments among several different asset classes. Typical asset classes might be U.S. stocks, U.S. bonds, foreign stocks, U.S. treasury notes, etc. Designed to achieve good returns by diversifying investments among several asset classes.

Asset: In financial terms, an asset is ownership of anything that has financial value. Assets include homes, bank accounts, common stock, bonds, mutual funds, etc.

Automatic Payroll Deduction: A plan in which a company automatically deducts a certain amount from each paycheck. Typically used for employees to contribute to 401(K) plans, company stock purchase plans, etc.

Automatic Bank Account Deduction: An automatic deduction plan where an individual authorizes a company to a automatically deduct a fixed amount from their bank account each month. Typically used by individuals to make automatic contributions to a mutual fund.

Baby Boomers: The 76 million people born between 1946 and 1964.

Bearish: A bear thinks the market is going down. A bear has an opposite viewpoint of a bull.

Blue Chip Companies: Companies that are well known, respected, have a good record of earnings and dividend payments, and are widely held by investors.

Bond Mutual Fund: A mutual fund that invests in many different bonds.

Bond: A financial asset where an investor loans money and the original loan amount plus interest is paid back over time.

Bullish: A bull is someone who thinks the market is going up. A bull has the opposite view of the stock market of a bear.

Common Stock: Publicly owned companies issue shares of stock. Each share represents ownership of a company. Owners of common stock are entitled to receive any dividends paid by the company.

Common Stock Mutual Fund: A mutual fund that invests in common stocks. Typically the fund owns more than 40 different common stocks.

Commission Financial Planner: A financial planner who earns their income by receiving a commission from each investment made.

Compound Interest: The investor receives interest on their investment. The interest is compounded. Each successive interest payment is based on the original investment plus previous interest payments.

Credit Card: A financial services firm agrees to loan money to individuals to purchase goods and services. The individual must repay the loan with interest. Interest rates can be as high as 21%.

Defined Benefit Pension Plan: A company pension plan in which the employer is responsible for saving and investing funds to give retiring workers a monthly pension check.

Defined Contribution Pension Plan: A company pension plan in which the employee is responsible for saving and investing funds to give the retiring employee a monthly pension check.

Diversification: Commonly described as "not putting all your eggs in one basket". The more different types of assets you own, the less likely you are to be hurt by one particular asset losing its value. A commonly used method of reducing risk in investing.

Dollar Cost Averaging: A method of investing where the same amount of money is invested each month.

Emergency Funds: Easily available assets that can be used for emergency needs.

Expense Ratio: The per cent of assets that a mutual fund charges investors for managing the mutual fund.

Fee-only Financial Planner: A financial planner who earns their income by charging the investor by-the-hour fees.

Financial Planning: Developing and implementing plans to achieve financial goals such as retirement.

Financial planner: A person who helps an investor to develop and implement a financial plan.

Growth Investing: A method of investing. Assets like common stocks are bought if they will continue to grow in value. The investment is sold when the asset stops growing in value.

Index Mutual Fund: A mutual fund that purchases assets that simulate a widely recognized financial index.

Inflation: The phenomena wherethe price of goods and services steadily increase over time.

Interest Bearing Investments: Short term, low risk investments that pay interest to the investor. Examples include bank savings accounts, CD's, U.S. treasury bills, money market mutual funds, etc.

Internet: A worldwide computer network accessible to everyone having a personal computer, modem, and phone line.

Investment Club: A group of people who contribute money each month and determine which common stocks to buy and sell.

IRA: An Individual Retirement Account is a U.S. government program where some people can defer taxes on personal investments.

IRS: The Internal Revenue Service is the government agency responsible for managing the federal tax system.

Liability: A debt that is scheduled to be repaid in the future. Liabilities include mortgages, credit card debt, auto loans, etc.

Load Mutual Fund: A type of mutual fund in which a fee is charged each time the investor adds money to the fund.

Long Term Investment: Investments made for more than 5 years. Examples include common stocks and common stock mutual funds.

Market Timing Investing: A method of investing in which stock is bought when the over-all market is low. The stock is sold when the over-all stock market is high.

Money Market Fund: A mutual fund that invests in conservative short term assets like U.S. Government Treasury Notes or high grade corporate bonds.

Money Market Fund: A mutual fund that invests in conservative short term assets like U.S. Government treasury notes or high grade corporate bonds.

Mutual Fund: A company that receives money from many investors and uses the money to buy and sell financial assets. The fund issues shares to investors. The shares represent ownership of the financial assets purchased by the fund.

Net Worth: Defined as total assets owned minus total liabilities owed.

No-Load Mutual Fund: A type of mutual fund in which no fee is charged each time the investor adds money to the fund.

PE Ratio: This is the ratio of the stock price per share divided by its earnings per share. The lower the ratio, the more under-valued the firm is.

Performance Mutual Funds: A common stock mutual fund. The mutual fund manager attempts to manage the fund such that the fund return exceeds the return of the general stock market.

Personal Investment: Voluntary investments made by investors.

Portfolio: A collection of assets. One example would be an investor who owns common stock mutual funds, bond funds, and money market funds. Another example is a common stock mutual fund that owns 110 different stocks.

Price to Book Value Ratio: This is the ratio of the stock price per share divided by the book value per share. The lower the ratio, the more under-valued the firm is.

Price to Net Current Assets Ratio: Net current assets is found by taking total current assets and subtracting all debt (current liabilities + long term debt). Also subtract the value of any outstanding preferred stock. This leaves the core value of the firm and is called net current assets. Determine the price to net current assets ratio by dividing the price per share by the net current assets per share. The lower the ratio, the more under-valued the firm is .

Price to Sales Ratio: This is the ratio of the stock price per share divided by the net sales per share. The lower the ratio, the more under-valued the firm is.

Rule of 72: A rule of thumb to approximate how long it takes something to double in value. To determine how long it takes to double an investment, divide the rate of return into 72. To determine what rate of return is required to double an investment, divide the number of years required to double the investment into 72.

Short Term Investments: Investments made for less than 5 years. Examples include certificates of deposit, money market mutual funds, etc.

Simple Interest: The investor receives interest on their investment. Successive interest payments are only based on the original investment.

Social Security: A U.S. Government administrated mandatory retirement system. Workers and employers must equally pay payroll taxes into the system. Benefits are paid to workers once they retire.

Software: A computer program which performs a useful function for the user.

Stock Broker: A person who recommends which common stocks to buy and sell. They earn their income from the commissions generated each time an investment is bought or sold.

Tax Bracket: The tax rate applied by to each additional dollar of income earned. The United States has historically had a progressive tax system with higher tax rates applied to higher income levels.

Tax Deferred Investment: An investment in which taxes are delayed to another time. Often taxes are delayed on the original investment and any dividends or interest earned as well.

Technical Analysis Investing: A method of investing in which future stock prices are predicted from historical trends in stock prices or volume of shares traded.

Term Type Life Insurance: A type of life insurance which provides a specified amount of life insurance for a specified period of time.

Umbrella Insurance Policy: An optional insurance policy which increases standard coverages. Typically purchased to give $1 million to $2 million total coverage.

Unit Sales: Unit sales mean how many units or "widgets" the company is selling. Growing companies will have increasing unit sales.

Value Investing: A method of investment in which assets like common stocks are bought when they are under-valued. The investment is sold when the asset returns to full value.

Will: A legal document which defines how your affairs will be handled when you die.

Index

Theory, Efficient
Market, 61-63,
65, 89
Thomas Jefferson, 20
Thoreau, Henry David,
41, 77
Treasury Bills, 33, 34
Turn-over ratio, 72, 123
Twain, Mark, 34

Umbrella insurance
policy, 177
Unit sales, 177
U.S. Census, 84

Value investing, 178
Vanguard mutual fund,
27, 74, 75, 79, 80,
82, 87, 100, 102,
103, 104, 107,
108, 110, 123,
127

Wall Street Journal, 63,
66
Warren Buffett, 12, 40,
124, 125
Will, 178
William Butler Yates, 50
Wilshire 5000, 49, 50, 65-
67, 70, 81, 84, 90,
93, 105, 106

Yates, William Butler, 50

Notes:

Notes:

Notes:

Notes:

Notes:

Order Form

Internet Orders:

> Addition copies of this book may be
> ordered from Amazon.com at
> www.Amazon.com

Postal Orders:

> Artephius Publishing
> 1291 Latham Drive
> Watkinsville, GA 30677
> Telephone: (706)769-6869

Please send the following books:

I understand that I may return any books for a full
refund-for any reason, no questions asked.

_____

_____

Ship to:

Name: _____

 Address: _____

  City: _____State:_____Zip:_____

Telephone: (_____) _____

Book Price: $19.95

Sales Tax: Please add 7.00% for books shipped to
Georgia addresses.

Shipping: $4.00 for 1st book, $2.00 for each addt'l book.

Payment: Make check payable to Artephius Publishing

Notes:

Order Form

Internet Orders:

    Addition copies of this book may be ordered from Amazon.com at www.Amazon.com

Postal Orders:

    Artephius Publishing
    1291 Latham Drive
    Watkinsville, GA 30677
    Telephone: (706)769-6869

Please send the following books:

I understand that I may return any books for a full refund-for any reason, no questions asked.

_____

Ship to:
Name: _____

  Address: _____

    City: _____State:_____Zip:_____

Telephone: (_____) _____

Book Price: $19.95

Sales Tax: Please add 7.00% for books shipped to Georgia addresses.

Shipping: $4.00 for 1st book, $2.00 for each addt'l book.

Payment: Make check payable to Artephius Publishing